Table of Content

ACKNOWLEDGEMENT

First of all, I'd like to thank my parents, Reatha and Porter. I appreciate every sacrifice that you made for me so that I could continue doing what I love. My brother, Mike, set the best example I could have possibly asked for, and I am eternally grateful for that as well. I also need to thank my beautiful wife, Angela, and my children Adrian Junior, Aaden, and Amelia, for their unwavering dedication to me and to this book. Our family means more than I could put into words, and I can't imagine where my life would be without all of you.

I can't forget to thank my teammates, both professional and collegiate, who have helped me to develop my talents along the way. Last but not least, thank you to the fans who have supported me throughout this journey. It's never been about me, and this book is a testament to the support you've given me over the years.

DON'T DIS MY ABILITIES

by

Adrian Peterson

Foreword by: Tracy Ham

Editor: Elaina Robbins

Published by Imprint Publishing, LLC

ISBN: 978-0-9853614-9-5 (Hard Bound), 978-0-9853614-8-8 (Paper Back)
Library of Congress Control Number: 2012947760

For All Booking & Additional Information Contact Us info@ imprintme.com

Printed in United State of America

Looking back on my life, I know that I've had to make a lot of tough decisions. But one decision stands out in my mind as the most difficult. When I received an offer to play professional football in Canada, my excitement was only only dampened by one thing: I would have to tell Adrian's mom. Though on an ordinary day this would have been good news to her, on this particular day I was worried about her response. From my turmoil, you would have thought that Adrian had been in a horrible car accident, not that I had received the opportunity of a lifetime. I understood where she was coming from; not too long ago, I had made her a promise. Now I stood on the brink of breaking it.

Adrian and I had grown up in the same hometown and even attended the same high school. His family, his mom in particular, trusted that I would watch over Adrian once he reached Georgia Southern. I had held big hopes for him too, starting that very first time I saw him play. It was his sophomore year of high school, and I had traveled back home to watch the playoff game and root for my alma mater. It was a muggy evening, just like it always seemed to be, and my shirt was already sticking to my back by the time I sat down. The bleachers weren't very comfortable, but it wasn't long before my mind was focused on something else entirely. He was different from those around him, even more so than I expected. At the time, Adrian's brother, Mike, was already playing college football for the Florida Gators. I expected Adrian to be stuck in the shadow of his brother's success; whenever someone mentioned Mike, it seemed that Adrian's name was never far behind. But as I watched Adrian that day, I realized he had an incredible amount of talent. I found myself in awe of his performance, cheering loudly for his successes as the game progressed. He commanded attention on the field and stood out from his teammates. I knew immediately that when Adrian was ready to play college football, Georgia Southern would desperately need him on their team. At the time, I was part of the coaching staff for Georgia Southern, where I had gone from playing to coaching for the Eagles. I decided to get personally involved in Adrian's recruitment, which wasn't complete until I made one very important promise to his mother.

I WILL TAKE CARE OF YOUR SON.

When I made the promise, I had every intention of keeping it, even though I didn't consider it necessary. I'd already had the opportunity to watch him play, and I was overwhelmed by just how competitive he was. There was no doubt about it--his determination made him so successful. On the field, he knew he was going to get the ball, and that no one would be able to stop him. In his life, he applied the same philosophy. Adrian was up for the challenge, whatever it was. He didn't need my help in order to be successful at Georgia Southern. Still, I made the promise to take care of him and watch out for him. Of course, I had no way of knowing that only a few weeks after his semester started, I would receive an offer to play professional football in Canada. My heart was torn. While I wanted to fulfill my promise to Adrian's mother, there was so much at stake for my family with this new opportunity. Before I even told my family about the offer, I picked up the phone to call Adrian's mom. I spoke to his dad first. I tried to explain that I had received this amazing opportunity that I didn't want to refuse, but that I had to call and talk with them first. I didn't want to leave Adrian at Georgia Southern by himself, but I knew that he would do all right without me. Success waited in store for him in the future, with or without me on the staff at his university. "I understand, but you're going to have to explain that to my wife," he told me as he handed off the phone. I took a big gulp of air and tried to be brave for what I knew was coming. "Who's going to take care of my baby?" she started in, angry before I could even begin to explain. She had already overheard the conversation and was ready to tell me just what she thought of me for breaking my promise to her. I really did understand her point of view. It wasn't that she worried Adrian didn't have the ability to perform, but she wanted to make sure he would be all right on his own so far away from home. He had struggled with his impairment throughout his life, and she worried a little bit more about that now that she couldn't take care of him herself. That phone call was the hardest I've ever had to make, and in the end she was still angry with me for my decision. Adrian knew that getting me off the hook with his mom would prove difficult at best. She couldn't stop me from signing the contract (though I'm sure she would have liked to). To this day, I like to think that I was secretly responsible for Adrian's incredible success. He didn't want me to get in trouble with his mom, and we both knew that if he didn't succeed, she was going to come after me. So, naturally, he stepped it up and transformed into an unbelievable player to save my hide. In all seriousness, I've been privileged to watch Adrian's journey from such a close perspective. We grew up in the same area, always knowing each other. I saw his talent gradually progress over the years. It was exciting on so many different levels to watch as he matured as a friend and an athlete. He had greatness written all over him from the very beginning because he was willing to work for it; and he never let the things that he wasn't as proficient at keep him from being successful. His entire family supported him wholeheartedly as he worked and sweated in order to make it to where he wanted to go. When Adrian's brother went on to become a great player, I feared that Adrian would get caught in his shadow. Instead, I watched as Adrian emerged from underneath Mike's wings to begin his own unique journey. He grew from a tentative freshman player for the Eagles to a dynamic powerhouse who broke all of the college records. Coaches raved about his work ethic. Others loved to play alongside him because he was the kind of teammate you wanted.

Being drafted into the NFL was part of a long journey for Adrian, one that spoke volumes of his determination and perseverance. Instead of stepping back and allowing his impairment to hinder his progress, Adrian used it to propel him further along in his life. We remain close friends even today, after Adrian made the switch from holding a football to holding his newborn children. Now he's changing diapers for his three kids, just like the rest of us do.

Adrian might not have had the easiest road to travel, but he had dreams just like everyone else did. When I first found out that Adrian was writing this book, I couldn't have been more proud. His story is one of the greatest that I've ever heard. It's one that people should know and read about. It goes beyond just holding a football, and it can speak to everyone. Adrian shows that it is possible to reach your dreams if you're willing to work for it. He teaches me that every single day, and I'm blessed to be able to call him my friend.

Chapter 1

Opening Up

"BEAR DOWN, CHICAGO BEARS!" The thunderous roar of the crowd was deafening, reverberating within my helmet. My heart started to pound faster, competing with the applause and screams that surrounded me. Everywhere I looked a camera flashed, the bright lights of fame following every move I made. It was nothing like Friday night football. This was the real deal.

The field that stood before me was greener than any I had seen before. The white lines were painted perfectly so that each camera could capture every detail and then broadcast it to the millions of viewers watching from the comfort of their living rooms. My cleats sank deep into the terrain, already trying to gain traction as we crossed the field from the sidelines into our starting positions. The jets flew high overhead, their rumble joining the last few stanzas of the Star-Spangled Banner. I tilted my head back, craning my neck to get a better view of what was going on around me. I didn't want to miss a single moment.

As we walked across the field, I remembered all of the Superbowl parties that my dad threw for his friends. We would all sit around the television, each person picking a team. We would yell and cheer, munching on hot wings and chips while we settled back on the couches and spread out across the floor. Snacks always overflowed from the coffee table, sure to create a mess later, but that never bothered us. Good-natured bets and jeers were tossed around as adults discussed the finer points of the game. This year, I knew my family was out in the crowds somewhere, but I could picture other families having the same type of parties that we had in years past.

EXCEPT THIS TIME, THEY WERE ALL WATCHING ME.

As I stood in my position, I couldn't help but think of all the days I had spent working toward this one moment. Summer days spent playing football in the humid Florida air rushed through my mind. My older brother, Mike, and the rest of the guys helped me to develop my first love for the game. I bet they never imagined that I would come this far with it. We spent so many days on those tiny neighborhood fields, fields that were nothing in comparison to where I stood now--the biggest stage in the world, the Superbowl.

I tried to center myself and bring my mind back to the game. It was finally time to start, and I hunched over into position. My heart beat a little faster with the excitement and nervousness that only football can bring to me. I prayed for confidence, for strength, for speed, but most importantly for health. Finally ready, I lifted my head up to look my opponent in the eyes.

KICKOFF TIME.

No time at all seemed to have passed from the moment we left the locker room. I wasn't prepared for everything that was going to happen. I still needed to let the reality sink in, but time had run out. I took a deep breath and had faith that my preparation was ample for the task at hand. The whistle sounded and I watched the ball arch through the air, though I hadn't heard the smack of the kicker's foot on the ball over the screams of the crowd. The football traveled deep into the field and landed into the hands of our pro-bowl kick returner. In that moment, it hit me: this was real.

Before I knew it, the ball was in my hands. The leather slid against my fingertips as I tucked the ball underneath my arm and ran down the field, adrenaline pumping through my veins. I was running across the field of a childhood dream come true. *Isn't it funny how things work out?* I thought to myself before turning back to the game.

I'd always shown talent on the field, but growing up, I didn't think fame and fortune were in the cards for me. While I first noticed my disability as a young child, I wasn't quite sure what to make of it until I was much older. Though I had once thought it would be my downfall, in that moment, with the wind whistling by my ears, I knew that my disability no longer determined what I would or could do with my life, But perhaps more importantly, I knew that I had to share my story and empower others as well.

I didn't even notice I was different until I was almost six years old. I still hadn't learned exactly what "normal" meant. Years passed by and my quirk slowly grew more and more obvious until classmates, church members, and even strangers took note. Each day was a fight to express myself, and I didn't know how to cope with the challenges that life had thrown at me. As time progressed, my self-esteem shrank until I found it tough to imagine making it through another year of school and therapy. I dreaded hearing the teasing and laughing of my classmates, for whom communication seemed so effortless. I hated being the one singled out. In time, though, I discovered that being singled out was more a blessing than a curse, as I reaped the benefits of my God-given abilities.

My story is the story of every child who has something to overcome in life. Though I dealt with a speech impediment throughout my childhood and into adulthood, it has no effect on the life I'm living now. My refusal to use my disability as an excuse has helped me move past my stutter and into success. When someone chooses to focus on my disability, they are truly "dissing" my abilities. God's blessings in my life shine through, illuminating far more than the inherent imperfections.

Life started much the same for me as it did for countless other children. On July 1, 1979, I was born to two incredible parents. As Porter and Reatha Peterson anxiously awaited the arrival of their second child, my older brother, Mike, was eager to meet his little brother. My father says that after my mom was rushed to the hospital, he sat in the waiting room, praying that everything would be all right. He is a great man who has always loved his family deeply, and I can imagine the things he felt that day. He probably didn't want to seem nervous, but no parent can help feeling nervous at the birth of a child.

I'm told that my father's face lit up when the doctor called him in to stay with my mother during the birth. I can almost taste his excitement at getting to be with his wife on yet another of their most important days. He stood by and held my mother's hand as she delivered me, their second healthy baby boy.

As the clock rounded 6:30 p.m., we officially became a family of four. My parents had already picked out my name--Adrian Nicholas Peterson. My screams bounced off the walls as I came into the world, ready for life. I'm sure my parents checked to make sure I turned out all right. They wanted to know if I had ten toes, ten fingers, two arms, and two legs. Did my face look the way it was supposed to? My mom likely surveyed her newborn and whispered a quick thank you to Jesus for entrusting her with yet another child. My father, usually both proud and strong, admits he let a few tears fall. They had no way of knowing that my disability would surface in a few short years. To have a physically healthy baby was more than enough for them.

My brother, Mike, remembers what it was like in those early days to have a new baby brother. In our family, being an older sibling was a privilege. It was impressed upon all of us that our new younger brothers and sisters were a joy to us, a blessing. Mike, therefore, never had those feelings of jealousy that often come with a new baby. Mike loved spending time with me when we were younger, and he would often tote me around and let me hang out with his friends. I was *his* baby brother; he wanted to take care of me.

When I was younger, I didn't realize just how different our approach was. I would see friends exclude their younger siblings from playing with us, which always felt wrong to me. After my younger brother, Rodney, and my sister, Lakesha, were born, I acted the same way toward them that Mike did toward me. I relished the opportunity to take care of them and teach them.

In those days, we were just an ordinary family. We weren't affected by fame. My parents had no idea that Mike and I would grow up to play professional football in the NFL. They didn't train us from an early age, pushing us to run faster and throw farther. Our minds weren't filled with images of grandeur. I grew up in the style of most kids. No pomp and fanfare, just a loving family who wanted what was best for me.

My first real memories take me back to Alachua, Florida, where I spent my early childhood years. Every day, my mom would take me to the daycare across from her work at Alachua General Hospital, the same hospital where she gave birth to me. She would wake me up early so I could get ready with her. I can remember the way her hands felt on my shoulders as she sat on the edge of my bed, gently shaking me awake.

"Adrian, it's time to get up. We have to get ready for daycare." My eyes never wanted to open all the way. My body was always too cold when she folded down the blankets, and I knew that when we got to daycare, she would leave me. Complaining, I would get up and get dressed, brush my teeth, and put on my shoes. I would sit on the staircase and wait for my mom to come help me tie the laces. As I sat, I often tried to drift back to sleep, leaning my head up against the stair railing and using it as a hard, uncomfortable pillow. I was always so tired it seemed I was getting ready in a fog.

My mom would tie my shoes, double-knotted so I didn't have to worry as I ran around on the playground later. She would hold out my jacket for me so I could slip my arms inside the sleeves. With her hand on my back, she would guide me out the door and into the car. Before the sun even rose, we were up and on our way to Gainesville, a twenty-minute car ride. The sky was hardly ever bright enough for me to really see the landscape, but most mornings I got a clear look at the stars as we drove. My eyelids would hardly stay open; I could feel gravity tugging down on them as I tried to stay awake.

I can remember sitting in the back of our black car, waiting to reach the bright Dunkin' Donuts sign. There was no missing it. Its white, orange, and pink colors popped against the dark of the early morning sky. The minute it came into view, my mouth would salivate because I knew what was coming. Almost every morning, we would stop inside to order our breakfasts. The aroma of freshly baked donuts and brewing coffee always filled my nose as my mom pushed open the heavy glass doors. I would stare in awe at the different types of donuts on display behind the counter, trying to pick which one I wanted.

"Adrian, tell the man which one you want," she would say. Unable to read yet, I would simply point until he guessed the right one. I would watch him wrap it in the baking sheet and nestle it inside the bag. He always handed the bag directly to me but gave everything else to my mom. I used to crinkle the bag, pleased with the sound it would make in my small hands.

"Say goodbye," my mom always instructed me with a smile. My parents constantly tried to teach us how to behave in public, to be polite and respectful to everybody. Even though I was only four years old, she tried to train me for the days ahead.

We would walk back through the parking lot, with me dragging my feet. I knew the next stop was the daycare and I wanted to prolong the minutes I had left with my mom. The gravel would shift and slide beneath my feet as she tried to hurry me up so we wouldn't be late. Eventually, she would load me back into the car, donut in hand and orange juice in my cup holder.

"Please try not to make a mess all over the car." I would nod, my mouth full of fluffy breading. This early in the morning, it was still hot from the oven. Happily, I sat quietly and munched on my breakfast. The donut made waking up so early worthwhile. When we finally pulled up to the daycare, my mom parked her car so she could walk me inside and drop me off. Instinctively I would reach up for her hand, certain that if I held on tight enough, she wouldn't leave.

Because my mom's shift started so early, I was always the first child at daycare. Usually, I was even inside before most of the staff arrived. This made my mother's departure especially hard. As she tried to sneak back out to go to work, there was nothing to distract me, only silence. I would cry and cling to her, hoping to change her mind. My tears would dot her uniform pants, making splashes of dark color. When I thought I had ruined her clothes, I only cried harder. In my mind, I was persuading her to take me away for a fun day at home. At first, I felt devastated each time she left, but I slowly grew used to her walking out of the building each morning. As with most children, my separation anxiety eased the longer we kept up the routine.

Playing by myself didn't interest me, so I would sit down inside and wait. I would rest my head on the table and doze off. As new children arrived, the clamor over their parents' departures awakened me. I grew used to hearing them face their own separation anxieties.

When new kids came, the excitement would energize me. In the mornings, I'm sure we played board games and chased each other around the room. Little kids can make a game out of nothing, and we were no different. But I do remember the best part of the day was going outside to play. As a group, we would all race to the swing set, fighting over who got to take a turn first. We would swing as high as we could, certain that with just a little more height we could touch the sky. I loved the way my stomach would flop as I began each descent. The way the wind rushed at my back as I swung made it feel as though I were really flying. People would walk by and smile at us as we played our hearts out the way only small children can.

After that excitement, we got to go inside to take our morning naps. No sooner would I settle in on my hard mat on the floor than someone would come and tell me to get ready to go. I loved being woken up from my nap to find my mother there, smiling. Because she dropped me off at the daycare so early, we often left before everyone else as well. It didn't make a difference to me. I was excited to go back home, even though I had fun with the other kids all day. Even back then, I enjoyed making new friends, something that would grow so much harder for me after my disability reared its ugly head.

When I was this young, my speech impediment didn't limit me. Young children often find themselves searching for the right word, having difficulty communicating their thoughts because they're so new to it. After all, it hadn't been long since I had learned to form sentences. My disability wouldn't become painfully obvious for a few more years.

Children see the world differently than adults do. They didn't make fun of me for my slow speech or the way I sometimes got stuck on certain words. We all just assumed it was normal for kids to not know the right words. As we age, however, we tend to pass more judgment on people. We lose sight of people's capabilities for studying the ways in which they fall short. Around the time I was eight years old, people began to overlook the things I was proficient in because they could only hear my stutter resounding in their ears.

My family had difficulty discerning my disability. It was something that I'd had pretty much from the time I started talking. Mike often said my stutter was so much a part of me that it was hard to imagine me without it. When you hear something every day, you begin to think that it's normal, and you overlook it. My parents had some indication that I was different because they knew what speech was supposed to sound like coming from a child's mouth, thanks to Mike. But I was different, a fact that became painfully apparent as school approached.

CHAPTER 2

Early On

As my daycare days came to an end, I found myself unsure about what would happen in the years to come. I desperately wanted to go back to those early morning car rides with my mom. I missed tasting the chocolate frosting on my donuts in the morning. What if I never got to see my friends again? Worries plagued me until it finally came time to face the unknown and move forward, as all kids do.

I was nervous, in part because I didn't have any friends at school. I cringed at the idea of sitting in class alone in the morning. A couple kids in our neighborhood were my age, but that didn't mean we would be in the same class. What if we weren't? No familiar faces would greet me and invite me to sit with them. What if I didn't like anybody in my new class? I would still have to stay with them all day long.

My older brother seemed so much cooler than I felt. He didn't worry about the day ahead. He was going to be a fourth grader and he already knew who his friends were. Mike has always had this contagious personality that everyone, including me, feels drawn to. Even then, his confidence was hard to ignore; and he had an amazing way with words. So while Mike ran around the house, excited to go back to school, I grew more confused.

The night before my first day, all kinds of emotions overwhelmed me. My anxiety increased tenfold as soon as I crawled into bed. I stared up at the ceiling, pretending that the imperfections made pictures, to distract myself. Forming stories for each picture helped me keep my mind occupied. Each time I let my thoughts slip back to the upcoming day of school, I would get unbearably nervous. Thinking about going to school made me sick. My body burned with nerves under the covers, and my throat suddenly felt like sandpaper. I clearly wasn't going to be able to make it to school in the morning. I sat in bed and made a list of reasons why I couldn't go, counting excuses instead of sheep. In time, I wore myself out with worry and dropped into a fitful sleep.

When morning came, I was finally ready to put my best foot forward. I put all of my excuses out of my mind and jumped out of bed, happy to awaken after the sun for a change. I stretched my arms up over my head, feeling the warmth of its rays on my skin. I decided I was done being nervous. I would be ready for whatever happened in that classroom.

Mike and I dressed in carefully selected outfits and laced up our brand new shoes. My fingers fumbled to find the holes, but I got it right with my mother's help. All dressed, Mike and I sat in the kitchen, picking at our breakfasts, too nervous and excited to eat much of anything. Even knowing we would be hungry again within a couple hours, we couldn't force ourselves to eat much. Our plates still sat full when it came time to leave the house.

The moment of truth had arrived: time to go to the bus stop. Once we got there, I knew there would be no turning back. As soon as we opened the front door, the heat and humidity of September in Florida washed over us, drawing sweat from my body on impact. I attempted to wipe my suddenly sticky palms on my shorts. A few other kids from our neighborhood had already gathered at the bus stop, and Mike and I joined them. Their presence did little to comfort me as I stewed in renewed nervousness.

We finally heard the growl of the school bus coming around the block. A silence fell over us kids as we each thought about what the day would hold. In a moment of terror, I considered turning around and walking back to the house. *I'll tell mom I'm sick,* I thought. It seemed like it might be true anyway. What little bit I had eaten for breakfast threatened to come back up. I looked at Mike, who didn't seem to have any worries, and tried to calm myself. If he could do it, I could do it!

The bus squeaked to a stop before us, the doors opened, and kids started filing on ahead of me. I put my hand on the metal railing to steady myself as I headed up. My ascent felt like a steep mountain climb, but somehow I made it. Mike had already sat down with one of his neighborhood friends, so I fell into the first empty seat I could find and then pressed my body as close to the window as possible. I felt the seat bounce as someone else sat down, but I couldn't bring myself to look at my mystery companion. We rode together in awkward silence until we finally reached the school. As we pulled up to the building, I attempted to steady myself through the panic threatening to overwhelm me. We were here. There was no turning back.

We had gone to the school the day before so that I would be familiar with my new surroundings. Looking back, I know it was supposed to help me feel more comfortable on the first day of school. It didn't work! I vaguely knew the room's location, but I didn't know what awaited me there. More specifically, I didn't know *who* awaited me. Mike, following my mother's instructions, met up with me as we left the school bus to walk me to class. Without him, I'm not sure I could have even made it into the building. My knees began to shake and wobble, and it took everything in me to force them to move forward.

As it turns out, I really had nothing to fear. As the first bell rang, I sat in my chair, just like every other student at Alachua Elementary School. The cold seat felt good on my feverish backside. At first, I kept my eyes focused on the table in front of me. But after the bell rang, I slowly raised my eyes to survey my new surroundings. The teacher seemed pleasant enough, and the room was covered with the colorful posters and trinkets so typical of a kindergarten classroom. It always offered someplace new for my eyes to explore.

My thoughts shifted to my teacher as she introduced herself to the class: Mrs. Laytor. We went over the rules of how to stand in line and how to treat our classmates. I sat there, uninterested in her words and yet fascinated by my new surroundings. After going over the rules, Mrs. Laytor played us a record, one we would be very familiar with by the end of the year. It would become an almost daily part of our morning routine. The music jingled in my head, and I found myself singing the simple melody hours later.

After our debriefing, we had the opportunity to introduce ourselves individually and get to know our new classmates. As I stood, I realized that my knees no longer felt like jelly. They had grown stronger and so had I.

"Hi, my name is Adrian," I announced with only a slight stutter. Proud of myself, I sat back down to hear the rest of the kids' names.

Mrs. Laytor then introduced us to one of the most important tools we would use that year: the color-coded station charts. We got one of these pretty schedules at the start of each day. At first, they confused me because I didn't understand how a color could represent something we would do. Looking back now, I can still remember what the colors stood for and how exciting it was to see the new schedule. Black meant nap time, which usually came after lunch or after our time on the playground. Brown meant we would curl up in bunk beds and flip through books, looking for the best pictures. But green was everyone's favorite. Green meant that we could go outside of our classroom into a little play area filled with balls and tricycles. We looked forward to the green cards, eager for the extra playtime.

When we saw the white card, we knew that it was time to go to lunch. We would line up behind Mrs. Laytor and walk to the lunchroom, giggling and trying to stay quiet enough to avoid being scolded. The lunch supervisor, Ms. Hall, did a great job of keeping everything in order in the lunchroom. She made sure she spoke loudly and clearly, something that really bugged me after my impediment became more apparent. If we didn't listen, she had a whistle that she wasn't afraid to use. On days when Ms. Hall was pleased with us, Ms. Laytor would reward us with some extra time on the playground, so we always made sure to stay on Ms. Hall's good side.

For two weeks, everything went smoothly. I didn't have any trouble fitting in. I was excited to go to school every day and play with the new friends I'd made. Nothing set me apart from my classmates until Ms. Brown showed up.

I had no idea there was anything different about me, but apparently other people had already noticed. Though I wasn't aware of it then, my parents and teacher had already discovered my impediment. Because of their realization, my class and I watched one day as an unfamiliar woman walked into the classroom. Mrs. Laytor looked at her, nodded, and said something that made me sit bolt upright in my chair.

"This is Ms. Brown. Adrian, she needs to see you for speech."

I was electrocuted, rigid with sheer embarrassment. I had grown used to Mrs. Laytor's class; we walked in line together, sat together, laughed and cried together. Now, in an instant, I was cut off from the pack. The other kids peered over their shoulders at me, curiosity glinting in their eyes. The memory of the pointing, snickering, and staring that day still sits crystal-clear in my mind. It was the first time I had ever been set apart, but it was far from the last.

In Ms. Brown's room, I would meet with the other two children, but we were never really told why we were there. It was comfortable enough; they obviously tried to make it fun for us to be there. There were beanbag chairs, plenty of toys. Games like Candy Land, Go Fish, and Memory filled the hours we spent in that tiny room. But it just didn't feel right.

I was never in Ms. Brown's class for the whole day, but I resented the interruption, no matter how brief. I didn't like being singled out, and I did everything I could to stop it from happening. Even though I always saw Ms. Brown enter the room, I would often wait until she actually came over to retrieve me before relenting. I was too stubborn to go to speech. It was willful disobedience at its finest.

We developed a sort of tug-of-war routine. First, Ms. Brown would walk into the room. Each time I glimpsed her ominous frame in the doorway, my eyes would dart in the opposite direction. If I saw her face, I was off like a shot, headed for the nearest toy. *If she doesn't see me, I won't have to go* I told myself. I would pedal faster on the tricycle, hide behind a stack of blocks, rush into a crowd of classmates--anything to escape her. Although her eyes stayed fastened on me, I judiciously feigned ignorance.

"Adrian, are you ready to come to speech?"

I flinched whenever she called my name. She had seen me, and now I would have to go. Unhappily, I would trudge to her room, trying to ignore the titters of my peers, to face the horror of Candy Land and beanbags.

I hated being different. I didn't understand that Ms. Brown was there to help me because I had no idea I had a problem. I thought I was completely normal, but my naïveté could only last for so long. My disability--and the divide between me and my peers--grew more and more apparent as the years passed by.

CHAPTER 3

Deepest Fear

I discovered my stutter in first grade. Nobody had to tell me that the way I spoke was different; I could hear it for myself. Other kids were talking fluidly now, and I struggled in vain to catch up. Though I didn't understand exactly what caused my difficulties with speech, I knew that I couldn't control it. The right words were always trapped in my head, unable to make the transition into audible communication. When they did come out, they were jerky and repetitive with gaping holes between each laborious syllable. Sometimes, the words wouldn't come out at all. It was glaringly clear that something was wrong.

From the beginning of that year, I expected someone to come pull me out of class. The first couple weeks of school went along smoothly, but I was a ball of nerves, anticipating being dragged off to spend part of my day with other kids who sputtered and paused as they talked. Though no one told us specifically why we were pulled out of class, we had it all figured out.

As the days continued to roll by, I began to think that maybe they had forgotten about me. I reveled in my luck at having escaped the dreaded walk of shame to speech with Ms. Brown. But my jubilation was short lived. About three weeks in, I was sitting at the crafts table, cutting out various shapes and gluing them. My hands were sticky with glue when I heard that familiar voice.

"Adrian, are you ready to come to speech?"

Sure enough, Ms. Brown's silhouette loomed in the doorway. She wasn't a particularly imposing woman, but to me she looked like one of the bad guys from my cartoons come to drag me off to jail. I looked straight at her, trying to telepathically communicate that no, I would not be going to with her, thank you very much. Her face held none of the resentment that mine did, though. She smiled brightly at me each time she came to retrieve me, despite my constant sour mood. In fact, she continued to smile as she ushered me to her room once a week for the rest of my time at Alachua Elementary.

In first and second grade, I could mask my speech impediment with relative ease. The other kids were still green, not old enough to be judgmental of my disability. We simply had not been around long enough to develop the cynicism that would haunt me later in life. Even though I'm sure there were times when my stutter frustrated them, my exchanges with my miniature peers didn't usually require a lot of talking, which made things better. Everyone, including me, would forget my stutter as we ran around the playground and enjoyed simply being kids.

My parents tried to set me up for success early on by putting me in speech therapy and encouraging me to talk, but their tutelage was not limited to me. They strongly believed that they needed to teach all of their children, in terms of not only the spoken word but also the written word. I remember sitting on the couch across from my dad as Mike held up the big newspaper in front of his face, hiding his small frame almost entirely from view. He looked like a creature made of just hands and feet and a crinkly newspaper body. My dad sat next to him, listening as the Mike-newspaper monster read aloud about sports and politics and new movies. I usually just listened, but finally the day came when it was my turn. Mike had just finished an article about a new shopping center, and I was absently running a toy truck along the nubby carpet.

"Adrian, why don't you go get the newspaper and read me a story?" my dad asked.

Nervous because I wanted to be just as good as Mike when he read, I swallowed hard and took the newspaper from him. Back to human form now, he looked at me encouragingly. *It's my turn to be the newspaper monster now*, I thought. *And I'll be a darn good one, too.* My hands turned grey with ink as I flipped through the pages, trying to find the best story. I must have picked one, but I can't remember what it was about. Thinking the words, I opened my mouth.

SILENCE.

I looked at my dad, trying to staunch the frantic feeling in my chest. His warm smile helped me relax. Feeling better, I squared my shoulders and dove in. It wasn't perfect, but I did make it through the article. After that, Mike and I took turns being the newspaper monster. I loved sitting with my dad and reading, regardless of how difficult it was. Back then, we didn't know why we read the newspaper, but we looked forward to it regardless. It was a time of undivided attention from our dad. We swelled with pride when he and my mother told us we had done a good job, and we felt sophisticated unfolding the newspaper and selecting a story.

When my speech impediment became obvious, it was even more imperative that my parents encouraged me to read the newspaper with them. It helped me to practice pronouncing my words. They knew I could understand them in my head, but they wanted to hear me say them out loud. My mom was a big fan of helping me speak as often as possible. She believed repetition was the best way to overcome any obstacle, and I think she might have been onto something.

With me working hard to form my sentences, my mom assured me that the hard work would pay off in the long run. The more I focused on getting my words to sound how they should, the more driven I became to do it the right way. Sometimes I would grow frustrated with trying so hard and getting very little back, but eventually my perseverance proved to be worth so much more than I had ever imagined.

Third grade was the hardest year for me. The gap between myself and my classmates widened every day. My peers were now able to talk and read aloud without much struggle. Their speech was smooth and articulate, their ability to communicate constantly improving. Unable to relate most of my own thoughts, I could not join in their enthusiastic chatting. This was not exactly conducive to fitting in, and developing deep friendships was out of the question. It was a horrible time for me; the only thing I wanted was to be average. Deep down I felt that they were normal and I was not.

My difficulties weren't due to lack of effort. I could hear the words in my head, and I *knew* that I could say them out loud. I could feel the syllables in my mouth and imagine how they would roll off my tongue, fluid and flawless. But somewhere along the way, they go lost. Certain words wouldn't come out at all. Pieces of others would come back, uninvited, in the middle of a different word. Sometimes I would get so frustrated that I thought it was better to keep my mouth shut.

The other kids, who were really beginning to take note of the way I spoke, didn't know quite what to make of it. They rarely had the patience to wait for me to voice an entire sentence. Sometimes they would fill in the gaps for me, making assumptions about what I was thinking. Other times they would just laugh and walk away before I ever got the chance to say what was on my mind. Whenever I was called on in class, they would giggle, anticipating my failure. I would shrink in my seat, wishing I was invisible to my classmates and immune to the constant teasing that embarrassed me and ripped away at my self-esteem.

The torment of speaking aloud didn't end when the final bell rang. It spilled over until my disability colored every aspect of my life. Ashamed, I tried to hide from it. I just wanted to be like the other kids. I wanted to be like my brother Mike, whom I looked up to. Why was I the one who had to be different? Why did I have to have a disability?

My stuttering was noticeable everywhere. My family went to church every Sunday, and we were always very involved. I liked church but I dreaded the big holidays each year. On Christmas and Easter, each child had to recite a speech in front of the entire church. I would spend weeks memorizing and reciting my speech at home. The words would roll through my mind day in and day out as I focused on making it the best it could be. When I was alone, I could fool myself into believing I could and would get it right this year. This holiday would be the one where I could finally say my speech without stuttering.

When the big day came, I would wait my turn in the pews with the other kids, trying not to wring my hands or bite my nails or do anything else that would reveal my nervousness. One by one, the other children, who had also worked hard to learn their speeches, delivered their words flawlessly and effortlessly. Parents would nod their approval of each child's speech, and the whole church would applaud energetically after each one.

When my turn came, I would mount the stage and walk nervously to the microphone. My mouth would open wide for a grand beginning that never came. At first, I patiently tried to force the words from my mind, but as things began to unravel, it became easier to pretend I had forgotten my speech. Each time, I could feel tears of frustration threaten to spill from my eyes. I worked so hard to memorize those speeches, and I was always caught between the desire to finish and the desire to run off the stage and have a good cry. Right when I was about to give up, I would look up into my mother's dark brown eyes, a refuge in a storm. She would mouth the next words of my speech, helping me get back on track. When she mouthed, my words would flow as calmly as a river. When she stopped, my nerves got the best of me and we began the cycle again.

The more nervous and frustrated I became, the more I would stutter. Stress seemed to trigger these moments of complete blockage. Pressure increased my desire to perform well, but it also decreased my ability to do so. Somehow, my disability left me unable to communicate the things I wanted others to hear the most. I wanted so badly to recite the speech as smoothly as my brother and friends had. I wanted to make my parents proud, as all the other kids had done. It wasn't that my parents weren't proud of my attempts. They knew how much I struggled and that I had a long, hard road before me. I wanted to show them that I could do it, to show myself that I wasn't different, and to show everybody else that my disability wasn't real.

I continued working with Ms. Brown throughout elementary school, but as fourth grade came to a close, I knew it was time to move on. The next year I would be in middle school, and she wouldn't be coming with me. My speech hadn't really improved at all, but I tried as hard as I could to make my dreams of speaking fluently a reality. In the meantime, I tried to focus on things that came more easily to me, such as making friends and playing sports. I had difficulty relating my own thoughts and feelings to other people, but I was still good at making friends.

"Why don't you guys go play outside for a while?" my mother would ask, exasperated with us running around the house. I was hardly seven years old at the time, but I was already itching to be involved in sports. Mike and I spent so many of our summers out on the football field or the basketball court, just playing. After our parents enrolled us in recreational sports that year, we began to play on official teams. It wasn't something they ever forced on us; as we grew older we started to see our own talents. I loved being on the field or the court. It felt almost liberating to finally be watched and critiqued on something other than my speech.

I wasn't always allowed to play with Mike. Often, on account of our age difference, he would play with his friends, but I would wait patiently on the sidelines for my turn. Though the team didn't look at me as a real player because I was so young and so small, sometimes one of them would call out the words I waited to hear: "Adrian, we need another player! You want in?" Nodding wordlessly, I would rise up from my seat on the sidelines. As I walked out on the field, I knew that Mike was counting on me not to embarrass him in front of his friends. I was always excited and nervous all at once, unsure of where one started and the other ended. If I did well, they might let me play with them more often. If I didn't, I would be destined to sit on the sidelines until I was old enough to join in again.

On some lucky days, I wound up with the ball. Whenever this happened, I took off running. I already had a love for the game. I urged my legs to move faster, ignoring the burning of my lungs as they tried to suck in the humid Florida air. Sweat poured from my brow and traveled down my face, blurring my vision and stinging my eyes. None of this mattered. All I saw was the end zone.

As I passed into the end zone, I threw the ball down with as much force as my small arms could muster. I had done it. I looked back at my team and was met with expressions of awe and shock. Who could have imagined that a kid four years their junior could be so capable? I looked around at all their faces, searching for one in particular. Finally, I found him standing close by with a big smile on his face. He had known that I would be able to hold my own on the field. He was my older brother, after all.

My love of sports was not arbitrary. Athletics were a vent my frustration. I focused on becoming the best that I could at basketball and football, trading my stuttering speech for stutter steps. In the classroom I struggled because I couldn't communicate, but in sports I was more than normal. I was great. My disability didn't affect me in the slightest. I was grateful for the distraction, blessed to have something I felt good about. But in the back of my mind, I always knew that my disability lay waiting for me when I got off the field or court, and I never stopped wishing it would go away for good. My wish was never granted, but I ended up getting something even better: faith.

CHAPTER 4

Conversations with God

My parents raised my brother and me in the church. We grew up absorbing as many intricacies of the Christian faith as we could. Each Sunday, we heard about how Jesus had died for our sins and come back, triumphant over death. The moral compass of the Bible was ingrained within us, guiding us to bring honor and glory to God's name through our lives.

My brother and I didn't mind spending Sunday morning in church. The church became an extension of our family, and we got to see lots of friends on Sunday mornings. We spent many hours worshiping and building a community there. I'm sure our parents were glad to see that we didn't view our faith as a burden, something to be cast off when we grew old enough to make our own decisions.

Faith played an even more important role in our household as my disability grew more obvious. Because we were raised to believe in the healing power of Jesus, we all thought that one day God would choose to take away my speech impediment. Romans 8:28 says that "God works for the good of those who love him." Surely he wouldn't subject me to a lifetime of fumbling over words.

As a family and as a church, we would often pray together for a cure. I spent many nights praying on my own as well, begging God to remove this seemingly insurmountable hurdle. I wanted to have faith big enough to move mountains, faith big enough to heal. The Lord never did choose to remove my disability, and my disappointment increased with each unanswered plea. I had a clear sense that God was ignoring me, and I could not understand why.

Frustrated by my failed attempts to incite a miracle, I looked for answers. I needed to know that I could overcome this, that the future held more for me than my stutter. I turned to the Bible to learn how others had triumphed over the giants in their lives. As I read, I was surprised at what I found. Within the pages, many people had overcome great trials and sufferings. They had enjoyed bright futures, and I knew I would as well.

My favorite Bible character was Moses. He had a pretty good idea of what I was going through, and he went on to do incredible things for his people. It was through Moses that the Israelites came out of slavery in Egypt and into the Promised Land. He even helped set the stage for Jesus's birth in the centuries to come.

The story of Moses starts when the Pharaoh decided that the Israelites had become too powerful. Forgetting a shared relationship from years past, Egypt was concerned with keeping these people under its power, requiring them to work under oppressors. Midwives were instructed to kill the newborn sons of Israelites, though some refused to participate. Daughters were allowed to live because they were not considered a threat. The Israelites mourned their losses.

One day, a woman gave birth to a son. She knew that her son would be influential in the lives of her people, so instead of obeying the commands of the king, she put Moses in a basket of reeds and sent him down the river. There, the Pharaoh's daughter found the little boy and, feeling sorry for him, decided to keep him. She sent a slave to find a Hebrew woman, one of the Israelites, to nurse the baby. Moses's own mother was able to reconnect with her son, to nurse him until he was old enough to live in the Pharaoh's house.

Through his mother, Moses learned about what had happened to his people. He witnessed first-hand the slavery and oppression they suffered from. As he grew up, Moses became angry about how his own people were treated while he lived in the comfort of the king's home. One day he saw an Egyptian beating his Hebrew slave, and, overcome with anger, killed the Egyptian. Afraid for his own life, Moses fled to a foreign land to seek refuge. Moses made a family in this land--a big accomplishment in its own way. It's only later in the story that we see Moses's speech become a problem.

Moses became a shepherd to provide for his family. While tending to the sheep one day, he noticed a fire raging on the bush, but it did not seem to be burning up. Coming closer to inspect, he was greeted by the voice of the almighty God. God had heard the desperate cries of the Israelites, and he wanted to help them. God had chosen Moses as the instrument to help set them free. Moses, astounded by God's choice and humbled by his own shortcomings, made a list of reasons why he couldn't go before the Pharaoh and request that his people be set free.

At the very end of his excuses, Moses says this: "O Lord, I have never been eloquent, neither in the past nor since you have spoken to your servant. I am slow of speech and tongue" (Exodus 4:10). Moses had slow speech, just like I did. His words came out haltingly, and he didn't feel he was qualified to perform the task set out before him. A lot of Biblical critics and scholars say that it's quite possible that Moses actually had a stutter.

Later in the story he says that he has "faltering lips" (Exodus 6:30), and that he cannot possibly relate such an important message to the king. I had faltering lips too. My mouth betrayed me each time my mind had the right words. They couldn't flow easily as my lips and tongue hesitated to produce the necessary syllables. I saw myself in Moses's predicament. I had so many things to say, important things to tell people, and yet I couldn't make the words come out the way I needed them to.

Most importantly, I saw that the Lord decided *not* to heal Moses. Instead, he provided another way for Moses to communicate with the king. He sent Moses's brother to relay his message. God didn't heal the man, but he made a way for him. Moses continued playing a key part in setting a nation of people free. He got to spend time on a mountaintop, surrounded by God's presence. He led the people to form a proper relationship with the Lord, and then got to catch a glimpse of the land that was flowing with milk and honey for the Israelites. Moses had it all--including a stutter. God made a way for him, and God would also make a way for me.

I kept reading, convinced that Moses's wouldn't be the only story pertaining to my situation. While he was the only one who also had a speech impediment, I found that so many other Biblical figures had overcome great trials.

David, for example, had a number of situations that forced him to rely on God for the security and answers he needed. Perhaps the most famous reference to David concerns his fight with Goliath. Israel found itself in a bit of a predicament under King Saul. Philistine, a neighboring country, wanted to go to war with them. They had already assembled all of their troops and positioned themselves in the city of Judah. The Israelites, not wanting to bow down in defeat, also assembled their troops and began to camp out and prepare for battle. With the Philistines boasting a great record of victories in war, the Israelites worried about what would become of them.

Eventually, the Philistines sent forth their best warrior. He towered over other men, standing nine feet tall. His name was Goliath, and he called out to Israel, taunting them as they cowered in fear. He proposed a plan for the Israelites: if they fought him and won, the Philistines would become the subjects of Israel's kingdom. If Goliath won, the Israelites would become the slaves of the Philistines. A lot hung on what was going to happen in a single battle. Given the intense pressure to perform, no man wanted to step up and take the challenge. They shook in their armor until one man stepped forth. That one man was David.

David found out about the situation with Goliath almost by accident. He heard about the giant on his way to deliver bread and other food to his brothers who camped out with the army. David knew immediately that he would be the one to fight Goliath and grant Israel its victory. He intended to show everybody that God was alive in Israel. The king argued with him, saying that he was only a young boy and he would not be able to defeat Goliath. If David lost, it meant slavery for the kingdom. They couldn't afford to lose.

But David had something to say. He told the king that while he was tending to his father's sheep, he would protect them from lions and bears. He would rescue the sheep from the beast's mouth, seize the attacker by its hair, strike it, and kill it (1 Samuel 17:34-35). I have to admit, it seemed a little bit strange that David would have fought lions and bears while he tended sheep. Sometimes God gives us situations that seem very unlikely so that we can be prepared for the tasks he will put in front of us in the future. I learned that God was going to prepare me to handle my speech impediment, the giant in my own life, and that maybe one day I would experience victory over it.

David went on to fight the giant without the armor that a normal soldier would have worn. It prevented him from walking and moving as he usually did and therefore wasn't worth the risk. Instead, he chose a slingshot and five smooth stones. The Philistine scoffed at the young boy who came unprepared for battle with a seasoned warrior twice his size. David had faith that God would deliver him, and as he slung the first stone, he hoped that God would deliver him and his people.

I saw so much of myself in David's story. I knew that I couldn't handle my disability on my own. I was unprepared for the battle, and there wasn't much I could do to force the words from my lips. God would provide for me in the same way that he had for David. If I trusted in him, he would take care of my every need. He would deliver me from my trials. Though he didn't choose to heal me, God gave me something much more precious. He gave me the strength to continue standing and fighting my disability, even in the face of the impossible. I see the truth in this as I stand today, with a great career and my family behind me, living a life that I never imagined for myself when I was younger.

David did get to kill Goliath and deliver the Israelites. They were so grateful for his contribution to their country that they desired to make him king. The only problem: they already had a king. Their king, Saul, had no intention of stepping down for this young man who had only recently taken the stage in Israel. He threatened him, and David had to run so that he would not be killed because of his popularity. David chose to follow the straight and narrow path even while on the run. He encountered Saul on numerous occasions and even had the opportunity to kill him and become king. However, David knew that he couldn't do that and still hope to maintain his reputation among the people and his good standing with God. He had no desire for retaliation or violence.

David waited until the Philistines again attacked. The battle was harsh and they killed three of Saul's sons. Saul, who decided not to wait for them to capture and torture him to death, took his own life. The people were overjoyed to hear that they would finally have the king they had wanted all along. David had no qualifications or entitlements to fame and fortune, yet God blessed him mightily with a kingdom.

In my own life, I asked God to bless my speech, but he decided that this wasn't the best option for me. Instead, he sent me blessings that I could not even fathom. As I child I never dreamed that I would be playing the NFL. He didn't give me a kingdom, but the success he granted me is close enough for me.

I also learned that life isn't always about God's blessing. It's not about the things we get, but about the faith we have in the Lord. I'm beyond thankful for the blessings I've received throughout my lifetime because I know my success is more than I could have done on my own. I've been entrusted with so much more than most people have; I have been in worse places. I know what it was like to struggle with daily life. The story of Job resonated with me because he too wanted to know when his trials would end.

Job once it all. He had a great family and tons of livestock. He was fairly well off for the time period he lived in. God thought he was the most righteous man on earth. Every morning, Job would make sacrifices, not just for himself, but for his children as well. Though he didn't know if they had committed any specific sins, he would make a sacrifice just in case. He wanted his whole family to be right with God so that their lives would be blessed. God saw what Job was doing, and he understood why Job was acting that way. Searching Job's heart, God found his actions and intents pure.

Satan saw how God favored Job. He challenged God to test Job by seeing how he would respond if all of his blessings were stripped away from him. Though he knew that Job would remain faithful, God decided to test Job and prove to the world that it was possible to live a righteous life even in the midst of trial. Job lost everything that he held dear. His children were killed when a building collapsed. His livestock was swept away, his servants killed. Both his wealth and his family were taken from him in the blink of an eye. Even in mourning, he asked that "the name of the Lord be praised" (Job 1:21). Satan decided that his intent was only for God to spare his own life, so he asked God to take away Job's health as well.

The next day, Job finds himself "afflicted…with painful sores from the soles of his feet to the top of his head" (Job 2:7). His wife begged him to curse God because she thought that his integrity was gone and God would no longer be watching over him. Still, Job remained faithful. Job's friends accused him of some hidden sin in his life that prevented God from blessing him, but Job knew better. He was righteous and they could not take that away from him.

Similar to those who offered me advice in church, Job's three friends told him different ways that he might try to get God to pay attention to his plight again. He mourned his losses and questioned God's judgment on him, but he didn't take his friends' advice. Just like me, he knew that there was nothing in his lifestyle that needed to change. He wasn't missing the mark, he wasn't straying far from God, and still God had pronounced this judgment on him. Over and over again, Job proclaimed his intent to remain faithful to God because he knew that God would look at his heart instead of his actions.

Eventually, Job received his blessings back, but he never forgot the trial. His children never returned to him, though he was able to have several more. His livestock doubled, meaning he was rich once again. His faithfulness was blessed, and he rejoiced in the Lord's proclamation of his innocence. In much the same way, I trusted God to heal me even though I never saw my prayers come to fruition. I knew that when the time was right, he would show me why I had been born with this disability. Job went through terrible trials in which everything was stripped away from him, but he was blessed for his faithfulness. Though I still struggle with my speech impediment, God has allowed me to live a full and complete life.

I remained frustrated for a long time because God didn't seem to want to heal me, but now I can see why. I never thought that he would someday use me to encourage others with disabilities. I'll never know why he chose me, but the Bible says, "Now we see but a poor reflection, as in a mirror; then we shall see face to face. Now I know in part; then I shall know fully even as I am fully known" (1 Corinthians 13: 12).

I want people to know that it is possible to live an amazing life despite your disability. I cannot know the full impact that my story has made on the lives of others, but I hope it encourages them just as the stories in the Bible encouraged me. God has a plan for every person. It is possible to move beyond that place of darkness, where there is no hope for future changes or successes, and into the light where opportunities are born.

CHAPTER 5

Struggles Mount

Even as my relationship with God became stronger, my relationships with those around me didn't go so well. The well-meant advice that so often came my way only made things worse. I listened to countless people from school, church, the neighborhood, and nearly everywhere else tell me how to fix my stutter. Much of it was unsolicited and unwanted. I would stand attentively, pretending to be interested, but inside I would rage against them. How did they know what would work? They had never stuttered a day in their lives! They had no right to suggest solutions.

I will admit, though, that I did try a few of the remedies. I even tried putting a pencil between my teeth while I talked, which one kindly churchgoer suggested (shocker--it just made things worse). I was desperate. Years of speech therapy had improved nothing, and God seemed to be ignoring me too. I needed to be able to communicate with people my own age, foster friendships and maybe even chat up a few girls, but every attempt left me flustered after yet another failure. More than anything, I wanted to start Mebane Middle School with a fresh slate.

Melbane Middle School was daunting. For one thing, the bell rang five or six times a day. Alachua Elementary's bell rang just twice a day, once to signal the beginning of class and again to let us know that it was time to go home. Suddenly, I was thrust into a school where each clash of the bell sent a rush of students hurtling toward different classes. It was nerve-wracking to be so uncertain about my environment again, and the stress didn't help my stutter at all.

After my first week of navigating the fray, a crazy hope that the administration had forgotten to put me in speech therapy began to bubble up inside me. I didn't want to repeat the whole Ms. Brown tug-of-war routine with some new person, didn't want to have to ignore the judgmental stares of the other kids. However, after that first week of freedom, my therapy resumed. I detested going, partly because I had grown to deem speech therapy inherently useless. I preferred to be in class, reading, learning, and passing notes to my peers.

I begged my parents to let me discontinue my speech therapy. I was going to be a new person, one who could learn to speak properly without being set apart. I tried to assure my parents that I would be fine without it, but they wouldn't buy it. As it turns out, they made the right decision. It wasn't until my eighth grade year that I began to notice the speech therapy actually helping. I slowly began to realize that hard work doesn't always pay off immediately, but it does pay.

I had to learn things that came naturally to other people. On a daily basis, it was a strategic game to communicate what I needed or felt. I knew I needed to overcome the continual struggle, but I just didn't know how. I thought I would never understand how. As a child, I had been pulled out of arts and crafts to learn a craft that most kids had already mastered. I knew I could run and jump like everyone else. I could even reason and think just like everyone else. I just couldn't let other people know what was going on inside of my mind. My teachers were sometimes unsure if I had really understood the lesson or if I had been paying attention, simply because I couldn't tell them the right answers. It was difficult for me to ask questions when I didn't understand something because the words never seemed to want to come out. My parents hardly ever knew about the events of my day. It's wasn't because they weren't interested; it was because I couldn't seem to tell them.

Throughout middle school, when even the most eloquent guy finds himself tongue-tied in front of the ladies, I noticed that my speech improved drastically when I talked to the fairer sex. This was a happy surprise, but it was hard won. My constant war with my words had forced me to overcome shyness at an early age. The rest of the guys in my grade were still trying to figure out a lesson I had learned many years before: true competition comes from within, not from competing with others on the outside. I couldn't compare myself to anyone else because I was so fundamentally different. So, while most of the guys in my grade tried to impress the girls with their premature biceps, I had no trouble walking up and striking up a conversation. What I did have trouble with was making friends with guys, which was ironic to say the least. I can't explain why, but I had difficulty even introducing myself.

The older I got, the more strategies I developed to manage my stuttering. Certain words got stuck more often than others, so I learned to avoid them. For example, the word "can" was usually a hard one for me, so while others asked "Can I go to the bathroom?" I would ask "May I go to the bathroom?"--which, of course, is grammatically correct anyway. If my replacement word turned out to be problematic, however, I was out of luck. My stuttering would become even worse and I would usually give up, leaving my thoughts in my head where they were whole and safe.

Oral reports were the worst for me. Public speaking makes almost everyone anxious. Some people tremble, others sweat profusely. The especially meek tend to end up retching into the nearest toilet, wishing they had never been born. But my terror was something different entirely. I had a real disability to contend with, one that made every speech and book report a living nightmare. I recall one presentation in particular because it was one of the most embarrassing moments of my young life.

Our English teacher, Ms. Agerton, had assigned each of us a presentation based on a book we had read. I read the book and I knew the material, but I somehow forgot about the presentation portion until the night before. I stood for hours in front of the mirror, practicing and praying that someone else would go before me and mess up horribly. That way, my presentation wouldn't seem as awful.

With all of the stress hanging over me, I'm surprised I slept at all the night before. I panicked throughout my other classes, focused only on whether or not I would give my presentation that day. It was hard to determine whether I was nervous about speaking or afraid to stutter, but either way my emotions ran high. A lot of kids in that class had transferred from other elementary schools and had no idea that I stuttered. I was still holding out hope that they would never figure it out.

I begin to pray again, not for someone to screw up, but for God to let me present that day. Another night filled with dread might make the situation even worse, I thought. I sat still through class, hoping my name will be called. It wasn't. I spend another day standing in abject horror in front of my mirror, mouthing words and imagining everything that could go wrong. I was right; it did make things worse.

Day two came. I knew I couldn't possibly take another night of sitting around. I sat at my desk with my fingers crossed and my eyes squeezed shut, waiting for my name.

"Adrian Peterson."

Finally, it was my turn. Although the extra night of preparation had drained me, I knew my speech well because of it. I walked to the front of the classroom with my head held high. I knew what I was going to say word-for-word. I could say it up and down, sideways, backward and forward.

The first couple of words flowed with ease, but then I started to get stuck. This is called a blockage, and blockages cause tension. The more I tense up, the worse my stutter gets. The vicious cycle had begun. Battles between my mind and mouth raged inside me. As my brain told me to stop, my heart told me to keep trying. I knew this speech. *I knew it.* All I had to do was get it out.

"Take all the time you need, Adrian," Ms. Agerton called. I knew she was trying to be supportive. She probably only thought I was a little bit nervous, that after a bit I could get through that miserable presentation.

I heard myself say that I would try again later and I slunk back to my seat, humiliated.

Did you hear that? I'm going to try again later, and I will not *have a problem this time,* I thought to myself. I concentrated on breathing, trying to stay calm. Other students gave their own speeches, which I could only half listen to. I wondered if I could eliminate all of the difficult words from my presentation, but I knew it was useless. I would just have to get up there and have faith that this time would be better.

"Adrian, would you like to try again?" The confidence that filled me during the first attempt was gone. I walked to the front of the room with my head down and shoulders rounded. I was a soldier ready to accept defeat. I didn't want to have another blockage, but I didn't know how to prevent it. As I started, I fought to force the words out from where they seemed to have taken up permanent residence in my mind. I stuttered over certain words and got blocked on others. My whole speech was choppy, but I kept pushing forward. Eventually, I realized that the end of my presentation was on the horizon. The excitement of reaching the finish line helped me end strong.

When the final word left my mouth, I breathed a sigh of relief. I practically ran back to my desk and dove into my chair. I could feel the stares of my classmates, but I refused to look up. If they hadn't known I had a disability, they sure did now.

As the bell rang signaling the end of class, the room filled with the squeak of chairs and the chatter of children. I passed through the door, a weight slowly lifting off my shoulders. I whispered a thank you to God that that was that only oral report I would have to give that year. And, after all, it hadn't been a complete disaster. At least I nailed the end.

My eighth grade year finished well. At middle school graduation, I received my second perfect attendance award. I went six years in a row without missing a single day of school. That was quite an accomplishment for me, because there were so many days when I was tempted to stay home and avoid the laughs of the other kids. Looking back now, I'm glad I didn't give in to that temptation. Though my self-esteem had been low during bouts in elementary school, the daily taunts started to lose their effect with time, and I developed a confidence no one else around me seemed to have.

Throughout this period, I stayed involved in different sports. My love for the games grew right alongside my affinity for both football and basketball. Sometimes I would be the shortest boy on the team, but I was still able to hold my own. God may not have given me the power of speech, but he sure gave me an ability to play!

My brother and I were both involved in different recreational leagues and teams, and we both played Pop Warner football in the fall. One day in particular really stands out in my memory. The night before, Mike and I had played an incredible game. We scored several touchdowns and executed great plays. The next day, one of the older kids from the Santa Fe High School came over to our house while we shot basketball in the backyard.

"Hey, are you the two brothers who were scoring all those touchdowns last night?" he asked, waving his hand. Mike introduced us because it was difficult for me to do it myself. We were so excited that an older kid had noticed us on the field. We looked up to the Santa Fe High teams, hoping to play on them one day.

That one kid's actions left an imprint on Mike and me. He encouraged both of us to continue playing, though neither of us had any idea how far we would go.

During my eighth grade year, I played AAU basketball on an all-state team that made it all the way to nationals. We traveled all the way to Seattle, Washington, to play in the national tournament. That taste of winning constitutes a huge turning point in my life. I began to feel a little more accepting of the person I was, including my disability, because I saw that I didn't have to be limited by my circumstances.

Though I still had troubles with my speech, my disability no longer ruled my life. Instead of defining myself by what I couldn't do, I fleshed out my new identity based on my talents. Once I gained the confidence I needed to look past the things I was struggling with, I really began to flourish in other areas. The difference from good to great is measured by the endurance of the individual to persevere. I had learned what it took to keep going and move forward, and I was on my path to greatness.

My parents never treated me differently because of my stutter. I still had to do the same things as all the other children. I recited my speeches for church, I gave presentations in class. My stuttering was attacked head-on, from when I was younger all the way until I moved out on my own. My mother would talk often of my two aunts who used to stutter. She told me that they eventually grew out of it, giving me hope that maybe one day I would be stutter-free.

One of my least favorite tasks was going into the gas station to pay for gas. The clerk would always ask what type of gas I wanted, and I always stood there with my mouth open, trying to form the word "regular." It was one of my blockage words, and it got me every time. Though I must have looked ridiculous, the clerk was always nice. She just took the money and ended our interaction. I would race back to the car, glad that the exchange, or lack of, was over.

Speech therapy had really begun to take a toll on me. Imagine sitting in a calculus class for hours on end, realizing more and more how horrible you are at math, with a teacher who seems to think calculus is ludicrously easy. Not only was it torturous, it didn't seem to be working. Frustrated with the way things were going, I spent most of my therapy time staring at the clock, waiting for the monotony to conclude.

The summer before my ninth grade year, I was fed up. I hadn't been able to convince my parents to let me quit in middle school, but I was in high school now! I felt sure they would see that I didn't need therapy anymore. I wanted to sort everything out long before school started, so when the opportunity arose, I seized it. My whole family had gathered around the table for dinner and I knew the opportune moment had arrived. I felt that my entire universe hinged on this one response. I knew all of my words had to be flawless.

Courage didn't inspire me to ask right away. I replayed the phrases I wanted to use in my mind, making sure they were perfect. I felt like a trap ready to spring, but no one else was aware of my tension. Plates began to fill with food, conversation began. For one terrible moment, I thought I had missed my chance. Then a lull in the conversation came, and I sprang.

"Mom, I don't think I need to go to speech therapy next year."

There. It was out. I'd said it. I could breathe again.

All eyes turned to look at my mom. My dad almost always agreed with her, so she had the final say. Moments passed, the clock ticked, and I still didn't have an answer.

"Go get the newspaper and read it to me."

My insides churning, I rose from the table. I walked into the living room to grab the newspaper, walked back, and then unfolded it slowly, selecting the article that would decide my fate. I studied the words in my mind, certain that I would be able to form each one aloud. Puffing out my chest authoritatively, I opened my mouth to form the first words.

Silence.

I felt betrayed by own mouth. I sat at the table, staring at the newspaper, willing myself to phonate. We sat like statues for what seemed like an eternity. My expression went from embarrassment to numbness until, finally, a single tear rolled down from my eye.

I was going back to speech therapy in the fall, no questions asked.

CHAPTER 6

Mama's Words

My mom always made each of my meals especially for me. Out of the six of us kids, I was the only one who was a picky eater. I refused to eat salt or gravy or sauce. Every night, I felt pampered as she prepared my dinner separately from everyone else's. Even though it was a pain for her, it meant the world to me that she took the time to accommodate my finicky tastes. It represents one of the most tangible ways that she showed how much she loved me.

My mother's love shone brightly throughout my childhood and the rest of my life, manifesting itself in every nook and cranny. It was the tender hug when she knew I'd struggled particularly hard; it was my favorite dessert, baked from scratch, on special occasions. My father was always there too, of course. Both of my parents had impressed upon me that, no matter what path my life took, they would always love me. They were there to cheer me on for almost every game, even when they had difficulty rearranging their schedules. My mom and dad both gave me the best advice when it came to how to handle the things life had thrown at me.

They were the calm in the storm of my disability, always guiding, praying, and seeking a solution to my stutter. I know they both worried, particularly my mom, that I wouldn't be able to overcome my disability. However, they refused to give up hope that one day it would no longer affect me. My mom always used to say that she knew God made everybody the way they were for a reason, but it was hard for her to see why I had to be afflicted with this stutter. Throughout the hardest years, she would reassure me day in and day out that someday I would be able to communicate with ease.

The one thing my mom did not tell me is that I would be normal. To her, I was already normal. Maybe that's why I loved her support so much. Other times, she had to take a tough love approach with me. I *had* to continue speech therapy, even though it was challenging and tedious. I *had* to learn to do my chores so that I could learn to live on my own one day. Just like any good mother, my mom made sure that I had the skills I needed to get through life intact.

My parents first noticed my speech impediment around the time I turned two. They were concerned that I wasn't speaking as much as most children around that age, but they couldn't figure out why. As I got a little older and started speaking, my parents realized something larger was at play. It wasn't until many years later that it dawned on me that I had a disability. I had a keen sense that the other kids set me apart, that they didn't want to spend time with me because I was weird. Looking back, I had plenty of friends, but in my mind, they sometimes didn't exist. In my darkest moments, I was convinced they were only my friends because they felt sorry for me or wanted to make fun of my stutter.

I was self-conscious, fixated on the things about myself that I could control. I would check to make sure I looked all right in the mirror every morning just so I wouldn't give the kids another reason to laugh at me. When I thought I looked fine, I tried to view myself as another kid would. If, then, it seemed my shirt was the wrong color or my shorts didn't match, I'd try all over again. It was almost as if by trying a little bit harder, I could fit in with them. But I was never going to fit in with them.

My mom knew that I would never be the same as my schoolmates. So, naturally, she told me so. Her pronouncement turned out to be one of the best pieces of advice I've ever received.

On one particular day in elementary school, I was called on to read in class. I stood and tried to choke through the paragraph with little success. The laughs and jeers of my classmates, barely staunched by the flustered teacher, still echoed in my ears long after the final bell rang.

"Why can't you just say it right?"

"What's wrong with you?"

"Just spit it out already!"

I was tired of being told to just get over my stutter and say things the right way. I couldn't help that my words wouldn't come out the way they were supposed to, and the teasing just made it worse. I had to sit in silence and take it, knowing that I could never articulate the retorts that resounded in my head.

After school, I got on the bus first and sank into the brown leather of a seat. Warmed by the sun, it felt soothing after the long day I'd had. Other kids began filing onto the bus, giggling and chatting, trying to push their way through the narrow aisle with their big, fat backpacks to find their friends. They would sit next to each other laughing and talking, telling outrageous stories of what had happened at recess.

"And then she tried to *kiss* me! Can you *believe* it? Gross!"

I could hear bits and pieces of stories from the seats around me, but no one came to fill the empty space beside me. *That's just as well,* I thought to myself. I didn't have the energy to try to have a conversation. The only thing I wanted was to go home and curl up in my bed, forgetting that today had ever happened. I leaned my head up against the window as the bus creaked into motion. My head beat against the glass with every bump in the road, creating a pounding sensation in my head, but I didn't budge. With each thump, my frustration dissolved further into cold apathy.

Once I reached my stop and made the short trek up my front steps, I was greeted by the familiar scent of home. I listened to the sounds of life around me and suddenly felt as though I would never be capable of being a part of it. I raced up the stairs to my room, trying to stay as quiet as possible. I didn't want to alarm my mother; I just wanted to wallow in self-pity. In my haste, though, I was about as quiet as an elephant. I was busted.

At first, my mom gave me some privacy to work through whatever was going on. Alone in my room, I dove into my bed. As the weight of the comforter settled around my body, I nestled deeper into my self-pity. The more I thought about my problem, the more exhausted I became. The pressure to do something about it--and the helplessness of not being able to--lodged itself right behind my eyes, making them water and sting. Before I knew it, hot tears created a nonsensical pattern on my pillowcase.

My mom's infallible maternal instincts told her something was wrong. I didn't hear her approach, but I did hear the soft clack of her wedding band against my metal door handle. I stiffened, trying to stifle my sobs and feign sleep. The door slowly creaked open and the light flooded in, throwing itself over my darkened lair.

"Adrian, what are you doing in that bed at this hour?"

So much for pretending to be asleep. I slowly sat up and tried to extricate myself from the blankets, wiping snot and tears from my nose with the back of my hand.

"There's a bright day ahead of you, Adrian. Let's get you out of that bed," my mom said soothingly. She grabbed my snot-free hand and led me into the bathroom, then sat me down on the edge of the bathtub. The cold porcelain shocked me into wakefulness. I watched, still adjusting to the light, as she pulled a washcloth out of the linen cabinet and soaked it in cool water from the faucet. She perched on the closed toilet seat next to me, and, with the tender touch that only a mother can give, began to wipe the remnants of my misery from my face. The cloth felt good against my burning skin.

"Now tell me about it," she said. "You just take a deep breath and tell me nice and slow what happened."

I paused for a second and took a deep breath, as she nodded her encouragement. Slowly, through stutters and pauses, my story unraveled. The kids at school had been making fun of me. My stutter wasn't getting any better. I was never going to be able to make friends or live the life that I had imagined. Tears threatened to emerge again as I recounted my tale.

"Why? Why me, mom? Why did I have to be born this way?"

She listened in silence, nodding her head. I felt her listening in a real, tangible way. Her reassurance and presence soothed my fears and chased away my doubts. Then she shook her head, and I braced myself. Time for the lesson.

"Adrian, you're *blessed*. Your speech impediment is *not* a disability. You have been blessed mightily by God."

Blessed by God? What kind of God thought the struggles I went through every day were a *blessing*? For a moment, I began to doubt my faith. I about said as much to my mother, but she continued.

"Adrian, it could have been far worse. You could have been born without being able to talk at all. In that case, you would have had to go to a school far away from your family. It could have been much worse."

Looking back, it's easy to see how in the grand scheme of things, my life could have been much worse. My mom was trying to open my eyes to the reality of the world around me. She desperately wanted me to see what everybody else had already realized: life could always be worse.

I know she was right, but back then I could only see the problems in my life. They were so many, and they were so big, that in my mind there was no way it could have been worse. I wanted to believe her, I really did, but she must have seen that it hadn't sunk in. So, for the moment, she decided to try a different tactic.

"God made you this way for a reason. God put you here for a reason. We're going to take things slow and we're going to go through this together, Adrian."

That much I knew. We had been taught in Sunday school that God didn't make mistakes, that everything had a much greater purpose. It's a hard concept even for experienced theologians to grasp, and as a child it was nearly impossible for me. Why would God make me this way? What reason could he possibly have?

My mom stood up definitively. I knew that she had said her piece. She wasn't going to indulge my pity any longer. As she left the bathroom, she turned around and glanced back at me.

"I'll let you think about that for a while."

I sat there, hunched over on the edge of the bathtub for what seemed like hours. I was trying to wrap my mind around what she had said to me. How could things possibly be worse? If you've ever thought about that question, I'm sure you know that you can come up with all kinds of answers. I thought about what it would be like to be in a wheelchair and know that I would never walk again. I wondered what would happen if our house had been hit by a truck. If I had terminal cancer, what would I do?

As each scenario passed through my mind, I realized that she was right. It could have been much worse. No matter what disability I had or situation I was in, it could always be worse. I needed to be thankful for the blessings that I had been given, not lament over that one thing I had not received. My mom was right: God had made me this way for a reason, and one day I would begin to discover why.

I stood up, my legs aching from being locked in one position for so long. I stretched them and suddenly felt ten pounds lighter. I had been given the life I had, and I was going to make the best of it. There was no sense in feeling sorry for myself any longer. I scampered off to find my mom, leaving my self-pity behind me.

What my mom told me that day didn't sink in immediately. However, over time I felt my life, and my attitude toward it, shift in a positive direction. My stutter held me back sometimes and it prevented me from really living my life the way that I wanted to. I tried not to shy away from opportunities that I knew would be good for me, but at the same time, I wasn't quite sure how to participate. In the end, though, I realized that my biggest problem was one I could fix.

My biggest problem wasn't that I had a stutter. It wasn't that people didn't understand me or that I didn't know how to communicate my thoughts. It wasn't even that I was a little withdrawn. My biggest problem was that I didn't believe I could really reach my goals. Instead of successes, I pictured failures. When I had to read in class, I stood up with visions of shame bouncing around in my head.

My disability wasn't holding me back. *I was.*

Great coaches have often told me to visualize myself performing to the best of my ability. If I want to learn to throw a little farther, then I need to see it clearly in my mind. Once I can picture what it would look like to accomplish my dreams, then I have the power I need to perform. Picturing it helps you to believe that it's possible.

Off the field, I didn't know how to picture success in my life. But in the end, you make the decisions; your shortcomings are just along for the ride. It doesn't matter what your disability is. If you have attention-deficit disorder, depression, anxiety, or any other disorder, it's tempting to hide behind the label. You can lose yourself to the disease, letting it consume who you really are. But as human beings, we are so much more than labels.

Deep down inside of all of us is a raging disability. It nags at us and pulls at our souls. We hear its whisper in our ears, telling us that it's not possible to go that extra mile to defeat it. We're all struggling with self-doubt, and when we're ready to rise above it, we can see just how much it's been holding us back.

I can relate my situation to football. Before I overcame my fears, I was playing on a nice fall day, and the air seemed to carry hope. This game could be the game of my life, I thought to myself. Hunched over on the field, I touched the soft grass and the cool, moist soil beneath it. When I was ready, I looked up and I saw the other eleven players facing me, dangerously close.

I could see that these opponents were different than the usual sort. The names on the back of their jerseys were unusual, frightening. I could see Doubt standing in front of me, helmet to helmet. His sneer told me that I'd never run past him. I'd never make it to the end zone. Inside, I could feel myself start to believe it. Doubt had eleven players, and there was only one me.

Doubt's teammates moved in closer and closer. As they approached, I felt myself start to sweat. I had thought this was going to be a good game, the best of my life, but I could tell that it was going to be terrible. Pessimism showed me his teeth, and Apathy threatened to take me down. Doubt's players become more and more offensive, leaving me cowering on my end of the field.

Timidly, I started to look to my strengths for a way to defeat my enemies. They were everywhere. Time and time again, I felt my body slam to the ground. The wind whooshed out of my lungs and Doubt hovered over me, smiling. He had done his job.

Growing up, this is exactly how I felt. My own self-doubt had become offensive in nature and the only thing I could do was succumb to it. When it came time to give a speech, my self-doubt said that I wouldn't be able to do it. But I grew tired of having to face defeat repeatedly. I wasn't willing to let my stutter tell me that I would never do anything impressive with my life. My stutter wouldn't define me forever. It could have been worse, and I needed to make the best of what I had.

"It could have been worse, Adrian."

Those words echoed in my mind over and over again after my mom said them. She was right. It could have been so much worse. God blessed me by giving me opportunities and talents, and I had to take advantage of them.

Post-transition, in my mind, I'm back on the football field staring at my opponents. They circle like wolves that have already had a taste of their prey. My anger starts to build up inside of me, burning. I feel it in every limb of my body. These opponents have held me down for too long and kept me from achieving my highest potential.

But this time is different. I don't want to just submit to Doubt's and his teammates' tackles. I am ready to fight back this time. Instead of taking the defensive position, *I* am going to play offense.

Doubt looks me in the eye and gets a running start toward me. I'm a running back, so it's my job to run the ball as far as I can during a single play. If he tackles me, it's over. I feel my heart start to beat faster as I make the decision to fight back. The muscles in my legs burn and adrenaline courses through my veins.

Not this time, Doubt.

I look over my shoulder to see him, lost a few yards behind me. I can't afford to keep watching him, though, because there are ten more players to dodge. I run past them one by one. My lungs heave with effort. My heart pounds in my chest, reverberating through my body. I keep my eyes focused on the approaching end zone. I can almost taste the sweetness of victory. I have to outplay everyone else on the field.

My demons jump toward me and try to tackle me, but my feet move faster than theirs. Ten yards to go. I pass the line that tells me I'm almost there. I've come so far, but I still haven't won. Being this close to the end zone makes me grit my teeth in determination. I gather a second wind and push forward. My whole body screams in protest, but it's not going to stop me from running.

Five yards to go.

I can count it in my mind. I can see the line in the grass for the end zone. Its whiteness stands out, and I train my eyes on it.

I DID IT.

One by one, my feet cross over the white line and into victory.

Perhaps the greatest game I ever played is right there in my head. The distance from good to great is measured by the individual's endurance to persevere. I defeated my own self-doubt and moved into the realm of possibility and success. When I decided to finally let go of my self-doubt and stop being afraid of achieving, I could see my God-given abilities. I no longer saw my stutter. Instead, I began to dream big dreams that would one day lead me right into the NFL.

I couldn't run away from my disability, so I decided to run through it instead.

CHAPTER 7

The Grind

In tenth grade, my dreams really began coming true. I didn't have aspirations of joining the NFL or becoming a professional athlete just yet, but I knew what I wanted out of my high school years. For some time, all I had dreamed about was becoming the starting running back on the varsity football team. I worked hard, attended every practice, and dedicated hours on the field to achieving that goal. I knew that I had earned the spot, and it was only a matter of time before others saw my talent as well.

The day I read that I had been granted that position, the one I'd always wanted, I felt so happy I didn't know what to do with myself. I reflected back on my days playing Pop Warner football with Mike, and I remembered the momentous occasion when the older kid approached us and told us we were doing a good job on the field. That was one of the coolest things that had happened to me at that point in my life, but this new triumph surpassed it. Both Mike and I had now been on the Santa Fe High varsity football team, and I was now on the same team that kid had been on.

I knew that a good season lay ahead of us. I would be playing alongside one of my best friends, Freddie. We'd played together ever since third grade, and we were finally playing on the team that we had always dreamed of. No matter how much my disability had held me back as a child, Freddie remained one of the few people who never noticed or mentioned it. He just accepted it as a part of who I was. We got along so well because we made a great team on the field, and our friendship spilled over into other areas of our lives.

The summer before the season began, Freddie and I traded afternoon pick-up games for grueling workouts. We, along with the rest of the team, lifted weights until our muscles gave out. We ran for miles through the hot, muggy air. Each night, we fell into our beds thoroughly exhausted from training in the sun. We hated it and yet we loved it. Each practice seemed more grueling than the one before, but we knew that the fruit of our labors would be victories during the fall season.

We also had some immediate gratification: our summer efforts were starting to capture attention. Everyone developed high hopes for us and grew anxious to see how we would do. Newspapers speculated about the upcoming high school season, some saying that Santa Fe High might be a standout. Some said we could be one of the strongest in the state. We tried not to let the speculations get to us. We wanted to focus on the game, our tactics on the field. But it was hard to block out the whisperings of potential that spun in our heads as we tried to sleep at night.

At Santa Fe High, there is a long-standing tradition of playing the first game of the season against the school's biggest rival, Newberry High. We knew that this all-important game would decide our fate for the rest of the season. As the date came closer and closer, the excitement and the nervousness seemed to become tangible. With each inhalation during practices, we felt the damp air gather in our lungs and buzz with a kind of palpable energy. Our practices became more driven, and we were more willing to get hit a little harder, run a little faster, throw a little farther. Our mouths constantly tasted like dirt and grass and our bodies felt as though they might fall apart, but we were getting better. Slowly the day crept up on us. When it arrived, we were ready.

Our last practice before the game ended when the coach handed out the jerseys. We would wear them Friday during school to generate support. Those jerseys meant a lot to the guys on the team, and I swelled with pride when I put mine on to go to school. I admired how it looked on me, paying special attention to the number 9 embossed on both sides. I was grateful to the coach for allowing me to wear the same jersey Mike had worn, honored to carry on my family's football legacy. By that time, Mike had graduated and moved on to playing college football at the University of Florida, only ten miles away. He was still wearing the number 9 in college, and I felt comfortingly connected to him in my jersey. I will admit, though, that part of my pride wasn't so noble. I enjoyed having people fawn over my accomplishments and know that I had what it took to be a Santa Fe High varsity football player.

Day turned to night and finally the clock signaled time for us to get ready. We piled into the locker room to get dressed and discuss our strategy. I was wired with nervous anticipation. As we took turns peeking out the door, we were amazed at how quickly the stands were filling up. By the time kickoff drew near, the bleachers were covered by a sea of people so thick that we couldn't see any of the shining silver metal underneath them.

Friday night football had begun.

The whole team concentrated on the words of the coach's speech, certain that they held the key to victory. Then we were ready to file out onto the field. As we stepped out of the locker room and into the night air, we were overwhelmed by the sheer force of the crowd. The band thundered, the deep bass drum echoing around the wide expanse of the stadium and mixing with the roar from the stands. My heart pounded in time with the music as I felt the anticipation of the beginning of the game. My hands ached for the feeling of the leather ball.

The cheerleaders had already worked the crowd into a frenzy. "Let's Go Raiders!" they shouted in impressive unison as we made our way out into the center of the field. The raucous clapping made all of our hard work over the summer worthwhile and gave us the spirit and strength that we were sure would fuel a win. This was the moment we worked for. This was *our* moment.

I searched for my dad's face in the crowd. I knew he would be wearing his bright white hat with the big red 9 stitched on the front. I finally found him in the crowds, sitting as close as he possibly could to the field. His smile said it all as we took our places for the kickoff.

We were supposed to be the best in the state. This first game, however, said otherwise. We fumbled the ball five times, and with each fumble, we grew more frustrated with each other. We were too excited to focus on the game. It didn't look like we would even have a decent shot at winning against Newberry.

In the fourth quarter we thought we might be able to turn it around, but in the end we couldn't pull it off. We lost to our biggest rival in our home stadium. It wasn't how any of us thought the season would start. The home team never wants to lose their first game, but more than that, we knew we were going to pay for it in the upcoming week. That night, when we thought we would be celebrating, we trudged home tired, sore, and miserable. It would be nothing compared to what we would endure at practice.

I got home and jumped in the shower. The loss steamed up around me, clogging my vision. Our team had fallen apart. As I worked dirt out of various orifices on my person, my mind zeroed in on the old adage "there is no 'I' in team," and suddenly I knew why. I knew that our quest for individual accolades and recognition cost us the victory. We were only there to show off how far we had come and what we could do, not to work together as a team. As I got out of the shower, I decided I needed to put it out of my mind and get a good night's sleep. I knew I would be exhausted for the rest of the season.

The coach was not happy about our performance, but his disappointment paled in comparison to the soul stirring I felt raging within. He pushed us to our breaking point, but even as we complained, we knew that we needed it. We didn't want to have any regrets the next time we hit the field. The new, tougher approach seemed to pay off, because we won the next nine games. We were untouchable, and we had locked in our victory by halftime in almost every game. We went on to finish our season ten-to-one, but we were far from done.

The talk around town was that the Santa Fe Raiders were going to make it all the way to the state championship. At practice, we were drilled harder and harder as we began preparing for our first playoff game against Crystal River. Though we were deep into the season already, the team's bonds grew stronger during that push. We started to rely on each other more, and we melded into an incredible team both on and off the field.

Going to the playoffs was nothing new for our school. In fact, Santa Fe High came to expect making it to playoffs every year. But this year, something was different. As the Friday of the game against Crystal River approached, our focus and preparation manifested itself in a gritty determination to win. They never stood a chance against our team. Our players ran up and down the field, free to run where we chose. Our defense overpowered Crystal River's offense, sending blitzes and tackling anyone lucky enough to have the ball in his possession.

After the game, as I basked in the glow of the win, a reporter from the Gainesville Sun, our local newspaper, approached me.

"Adrian Peterson, would you mind doing an interview with me about that amazing game?"

I froze. I desperately wanted to take this opportunity to share how hard our team had worked, how confident we were that we could continue this path all the way to the state championship. But this was my first interview, and I wasn't quite sure what to expect. Would I be able to have an intelligible conversation with this man? After momentarily musing on the fact that I was more afraid to talk to a reporter than I was to face burly football players, I swallowed my anxiety and decided to try my best.

Unfortunately, things didn't go so well. I stuttered badly on every word. The reporter looked confused at the discrepancy between my skills on the field and my skills with speech, but he was nice enough about it, which was more than I would get in some future interviews. I rejoined my teammates feeling disappointed in myself, though I soon forgot in the face of their joy.

That year, we won the Florida 4A state championship. That was one of the biggest turning points for my career. After our breakthrough, a number of college coaches and scouts began to frequent our practices and games. It was my junior year, time to start getting ready for college. Sure enough, recruitment letters began filling our mailbox every day. The team didn't manage to win another state championship that year, but we did finish strong. When the season was over, the phone started ringing.

The first call took me a little bit by surprise, but at the same time, I had been expecting it. Only a couple years before, I had seen my brother, Mike, go through the same thing. While it was still new and exciting to me, having recruiters on the line in our household had become a strangely exhilarating routine. Every time the phone rang, I would wonder if it was someone offering me the chance of a lifetime.

As excited as I was to hear from colleges, each phone call put me on edge. So many emotions swelled up inside me that the words would get blocked. For the most part, I would sit, phone in hand, and allow them to do all the talking. After all, they're so busy trying to sell you on their school that they have plenty to say. I dreaded the moment when I would have to respond. Would any of them turn me down because I couldn't even talk to them like a normal person? Though I had begun to embrace my disability, I still dreaded the reactions it garnered from strangers.

"So what do you think about that, Adrian?"

The question might have sounded a little different depending on who was calling, but the answer was normally the same. I needed a scholarship, so I was willing to consider whoever offered one. But that didn't always translate well when it came time to speak. I never seemed to be able to start speaking, and the silence was deafening over the phone. Several coaches even thought that I had hung up on them. When I finally got started, I had the usual troubles, such as pauses in between words and stutters.

If I was having a really bad day, after several failed attempts to articulate myself, I would begin to wonder if I should just hang up. After all, I didn't even know this person. I didn't know him and he didn't know me. And yet, I could still feel the judgment. I could hear shuffling on the other end of the line and could feel the disappointment as the recruiter started to think I wasn't the player for his school. The recruiters expected someone just as proficient at speaking as performing on the football field. Instead, they heard my stutter and immediately imagined that I might not be the right fit for them. In the end, sometimes all I could say was that I would consider their offer.

My junior year was a big year for me academically, because it all led up to one moment. Would I pass the ACT? That test stood between me and my future career playing college sports. In years past, I had heard stories of great players who hadn't been able to go on to play college sports because they didn't qualify academically. In order to continue to receiving scholarship offers, I needed to prove that I was proficient in areas other than the football field. I had to be proficient in math, English, and science as well.

As if that wasn't enough to scare me, I already knew that I performed poorly on standardized tests. I was intelligent and I brought home good grades, but I knew that this might not reflect in my ACT scores. When I sat down to take a test, I often felt the same way I did when I stood up to give a speech--like the ideas in my head were impossible to get out. I would question myself, over-analyzing and leaving gaping holes in the answer key from erasing too many times. I only needed a seventeen or higher in order to receive the scholarships and play college football, but I wasn't sure that I could do it.

The week before the test, I studied as much as I could. I was locked down with my study books and a pencil in each spare moment. Sometimes I would just sit, staring at the books that were supposed to help me prepare, my old friend Doubt looming over me. The books were so thick and heavy that I knew I would never be able to get all the way through them. My body would grow rigid, atrophied from my futile concentration. The words on the page smeared and warped until they were one big unintelligible mess in my mind.

Despite my frustration, I tried to keep at it. The Friday night before the test was the worst. I knew I was going to get up early, and my entire future seemed to hang in the balance. My number-two pencil, not my feats on the football field, signified the beginning of my upcoming college career. I tossed and turned in the bed, stewing in misery. I knew I had all the information in my head, it was just a matter of getting it out onto the page, not letting my panic cloud it. I tried to force myself to drift off, telling myself I would do better on the test if I was well-rested.

Eventually, my mind wore itself out and I did fall asleep. It felt like only seconds had passed when my alarm went off. I dragged my leaden body out of bed and fumbled my way through breakfast, only because I had heard that you had to eat before a standardized test. I don't even remember driving over to the testing center; the next thing I knew, I was sitting at my tiny wooden desk to take my exam. Looking around, I saw sleepy but confident-looking teens surrounding me. I wished that my expression matched theirs.

Sure enough, I had unconsciously invited Doubt's entire team to the exam. My answer sheet turned black with erase marks. I felt air seep from the room with every tick of the clock. While everyone else calmly took their tests, I had a silent, miniature panic attack. I felt like a little kid again, trying to stutter my way through a presentation while ignoring the jeers of my peers. When the proctor told us to put our pencils down, I shoved my paper away in disgust.

For weeks, I ignored the nagging feeling in the back of my mind that told me my life was over. The day the scores finally came in the mail, I came home to find an ominous white envelope sitting on the counter like an evil sneer. I grabbed it and, before it could bite me, ripped it open.

I had scored a fifteen. Two points below what I needed, and well below what I was capable of.

It felt like the floor had dropped out beneath me. I knew that I could retake the test the fall of my senior year, but I wasn't sure if I could hold it together, even with the next six months to prepare. When my mom saw my score, she tried to tell me that there was no pressure since I only needed an extra two points. Surely they would come easily the next time around. After all, I was already familiar with the test.

In the end, there really wasn't anything I could do about that score. I had failed the first time around, but there was always another test to take in the fall. I would spend the summer preparing. I would stop erasing all of my right answers and replacing them with wrong ones. I would learn to be calm, and I sure wasn't letting Doubt and his cronies into the testing center with me a second time.

And in the end, I didn't.

CHAPTER 8

Soaring Above

Even though I hadn't passed the test at this point, colleges continued to pursue me. I knew I would have to decide on one college, but that wasn't the only thing I needed to decide. College scouts were offering basketball scholarships. I was heavily involved in both sports during my years at Santa Fe High, and I had developed a love for both games. I needed to choose not only what school I would go to but also what sport I would play there.

Every school offered a great package: a scholarship, a good education, and a shot at being recruited into the NFL. I spent night after night in front of my computer looking up the statistics for each team, searching for stories about coaches, and watching tapes of old games. I was hardly even an adult, and I had to make one of the most important decisions of my life. The pressure to pick nagged at me but didn't bring me any closer to a resolution.

My parents made it as easy as they could for me. On Friday nights, we would drive up to different schools and spend a night experiencing the atmosphere there, talking to the coach and watching practices. Occasionally we would go out to dinner with coaches, trying to get a feel for who they were and how they ran their teams. On Saturdays, we would always tour the campus and talk about the academic side of the university. I didn't like that day as much. To me, a campus was a campus. They all looked relatively the same, with their beautiful buildings and well-maintained grounds. They offered places for students to relax comfortably, to socialize, and to pour over books. Everything seemed the same no matter where we traveled, especially since every school that offered a scholarship had high-quality academics. We didn't have to worry much about whether or not I would have a decent education.

I was primarily concerned with what the football team was like. In high school, my teammates and I shared a close bond that made us wildly successful on the field. Whenever I visited a team, one of the first things I looked for was how tightly knit they were. Would they argue over who had the ball or would they work together, protecting each other and encouraging one another to push their limits? I knew what true friendship on a team looked like, and I wanted that to be the defining aspect of the group I chose.

In the end, my parents and I visited every school on my list. I was able to narrow it down to only a few options. I spent a lot of time reading brochures and pamphlets as I tried to make the right choice. My mind would flip back to the teams and their potential for a successful upcoming season. A weight permanently settled in my stomach as I juggled pros and cons.

In the end, my loyalty to my family kept me from straying too far. My parents had always been there for me, and I knew they didn't really want me to go far away. My younger brother had just been recruited onto the high school team, and I didn't want to miss out on his first games as a Santa Fe High Raider.

I set my sights on Georgia Southern.

It was close enough for my parents to drive to Saturday games. If I had gone to a school farther north, they would have rarely been able to see me play. Rodney played on Friday nights, and then they could travel up to see me play the next morning. Wanting to have them there, I decided to stay as close as possible.

The minute I made my decision, it felt as though I had been lifted out of quicksand. I could breathe again. I decided I would tell my parents over dinner. Just like the night I had asked my mom if I could discontinue my therapy, I waited for that lull in the conversation. Except this time, I could barely mask the smile on my face.

"Mom, Dad, I think I've made my decision."

My parents looked up from their plates, preparing for what was about to come. I could tell they felt nervous, afraid that I would move far away where they would hardly see me anymore. I tried to keep a straight face, one that showed I was serious about this choice, that I was mature and responsible enough to make it on my own. I could tell I had everyone's attention.

"And what would that be, Adrian?" my mom asked. She sounded nervous.

"Georgia Southern." I smiled as my family broke into a round of applause. Both Mike and I had opted to stay close to home, and I knew everyone was grateful for it. My brother and sister grinned, knowing what a big deal it would be for me to go on to play college football. My mom got up from the table to give me a hug, her face shining with pride. My dad shook my hand firmly to tell me he was proud of me for the choice I'd made, that he knew the school would make a good fit for me. They had no idea just how great it would turn out to be.

That fall, when it was time to leave my family and start the newest chapter of my life, I felt the hesitation that most young adults feel. My mom and I went shopping for the things I needed in my dorm room, and piece by piece my college life became a reality. I remember looking around my room the day before the move, staring at everything packed neatly into cardboard boxes. My clothes were crisp and clean, folded perfectly, thanks to my mom. She had been preparing for days, trying to keep herself distracted as yet another of her children was leaving her behind to start a life of his own.

I threw myself over my childhood bed, enjoying the familiar feel of the old mattress. In a way, I felt like I had before my first day of elementary school. I didn't really know many people where I was headed and I would have to learn my way around. But this time, I didn't feel panicky. I was no longer the kid who literally made himself sick with worry. For the first time, I imagined all of the things that could go right instead of what could be disastrous.

I stared at the ceiling, thinking that in less than twenty-four hours I would sleep in a different bed. The thought left a funny, dizzy feeling in my stomach. I drifted off to sleep, excited for the next day to begin.

I woke up to the sound of my dad throwing open my bedroom door. Though I had set an alarm, it appeared that he was too excited to wait for it. Already, the sun had washed the room in glowing light.

"You going to get up sometime today and help me move these boxes?" my dad asked, smiling. He knew that getting up in the morning wasn't one of my favorite parts of the day.

"I'll be up in a minute, dad," I moaned, rolling back over and smashing the pillow into my face. My dad left the room, his laughter still ringing in the air. It wasn't a day of sadness, but one of excitement and joy.

I pushed off the covers and sat up, staring at the boxes. It was hard to believe that soon these boxes would be in the car, not to return for quite a while. My brother Rodney and sister Lakesha were already downstairs when I got there. We ate our cereal, bantering as only siblings can, until a holler resounded from the other room.

"Come on, Adrian! We need to get moving," my dad called, and I could hear the hustle and bustle of him shifting boxes around in the living room. I stuck my bowl in the sink and joined him, carrying box after box of clothing and games and books down the stairs, trying not to snag my feet on anything. For a while, I wasn't sure that everything would fit in the car, but somehow we managed it. By the time the doors were shut and everyone had squashed themselves in, the tail end of the car was a good two inches lower than usual. I worried that when we opened the doors everything--and everyone--would fall out.

It wasn't a long drive, but with five people and all my belongings in the car it was a little cramped. My parents, however, thought it was important for everyone to come and see me off, and my brother and sister, who were nearing college age, were curious to see Georgia Southern. Not to mention, the more people we brought, the faster we would be able to unload the car. Unfortunately, August was not only hot but muggy and humid as well. The close contact didn't help.

As the school slowly came into my view, my heart leapt inside my chest from a combination of anticipation and extreme heat. Georgia Southern was an impressive school, but most importantly, it was *my* school. We pulled into the parking lot and unloaded the boxes, each one of us carrying as much as possible. I proudly fished the dorm key, which had been mailed to the house weeks earlier, out of my pocket and slid it into the lock of my new home.

Panting, we all dropped off our cargo and surveyed the dorm. The other half was already occupied, though my new roommate was nowhere to be found. I took a good long look at the family members who had come. A pang of sadness hit me as I thought about them leaving that day, but when I looked out the tiny window of my new room, I smiled.

Welcome home, Adrian, I thought to myself.

Almost immediately, the football team was thrust together to prepare for the upcoming season. New players only had a few days to settle into their lives at the school before practices began. After all, there were weights to lift, laps to run, and scrimmages to play.

Mike and I often talked about what it was like to play college football, especially after recruiters started calling for me. When I looked around at my teammates in the locker room, I realized that what he had told me was right. The men around me were much bigger than the ones I had often played with in high school, especially the veterans. Their muscles bulged and twisted like vines around their bodies. It was enough to make me wish I had spent a little more time in the gym before I left home.

There was another big difference between this locker room and mine from high school. High school sports normally have a few key players, the ones who are serious about making sports into a career. Those players are the superstars. The others fall in line behind them to admire their skills and learn something from them. Now that I was at college, I realized that everyone around me was a superstar somewhere. They were the best of the best from their high schools, and they had been chosen to play on the same elite team that I had. In that sense, we were all equal. We all had the talent and the drive to make it this far. Our coaches only hoped that we would have the cohesive ability to play as a team instead of fueling our own egos.

I quickly spotted Derrick among the crowd of biceps and unfamiliar faces in the locker room. I actually saw a lot of Derrick that year, since our beds were about three feet away from each other. He had gone to a rival school, and I had grown up playing against him. It was hard for both of us to let our guards down and play as teammates after years of trying to outdo each other, but despite our history, something clicked in our friendship. We tried to help each other out, both on and off the field.

I told myself that the game was exactly the same as it had always been, so there was no reason for me to feel intimidated. Each time we made our way onto the field, I was determined to try even harder. We started our practices with grueling conditioning, heavy weights, and intense cardio sessions. My heart would beat faster than I thought possible--or healthy, for that matter--but I loved every minute of it. We rounded off every practice with a scrimmage to see how we fared as a team. It wasn't long before I caught on to the differences between high school and college football. The guys around me weren't just bigger than my high school cohorts, they were much better football players. They knew exactly what they were doing and what they needed to do next. It was a learning curve for me, but by the first game, I had mostly adjusted.

As soon as practice ended, we would all hit the showers and run to the cafeteria for quick meal. Then Derrick and I would head back to our room to relax and play video games. Our favorite was NCAA football, which we played on our old Playstation. Yep, even our video games were football games. I'm the first to admit that we were a little obsessed. With all the 'practice' we got, we both got really good, and competing proved a never-ending diversion. After practice, after study hall, and long past the time we were supposed to be asleep, we would be playing what we always told ourselves was one last game.

It seemed that we were always doing something crazy together, but I could never forget the night that we both realized God was watching out for us. It was around six o'clock in the evening, and I was particularly exhausted after practice. Derrick and I wanted to head to the Pickle Barrel, a nearby student eatery, to pick up some snacks. We went there a few times a week to pick up extra food and use our meal plan.

I let Derrick drive, not really thinking anything of the problems I was having with my brakes. My brakes had been problematic for a while at that point; sometimes they would work fine, but other times I would slam on it and it wouldn't do a thing. Like any busy college student, I ignored the problem and hoped it would go away.

My stomach growled as I tossed Derrick the keys and hopped into the passenger seat. I clicked my seat belt into place, unaware that in just a few minutes I would desperately need it. We laughed and carried on as we drove down the main street of campus. It was the busiest road around, especially in the evenings.

I saw the bright red of the familiar stop sign looming closer and closer, but the car wasn't slowing down. As I opened my mouth to say something, Derrick looked over at me. I knew something was wrong.

"The car won't stop!"

A cold sweat broke out on my forehead. I didn't know what to do. We were headed into the busiest intersection on campus and we couldn't stop the car. We weren't going very fast, probably less than thirty miles per hour, but there were no options other than to go straight through it. I gripped the seat I was sitting on and started to pray. I looked at Derrick, who had both feet slammed onto the pedal in an effort to slow us down. He was practically standing on the brake pedal, his hands clutched around the steering wheel as if it was trying to get away from him. The intersection came closer and closer, and I braced myself for an impact.

But when we got there, not a single car was in sight.

There were no cars in any direction on the busiest road around. Moments after we drove through the deserted road in silent disbelief, the car came to a screeching halt. The brakes had started working again.

Almost in unison, we breathed a heavy, "Thank you, God!" and took a minute to think about what had just happened. We could have easily wound up in the hospital, but instead we were safely sitting in the parking lot of the Pickle Barrel. We didn't have to say another word about it. God was definitely watching over us.

When the first game came, I was excited to see what it would be like to play with a state-of-the-art team such as this one. I flashed back to the giddy feeling I had my sophomore year of high school as I read in newspaper after newspaper that our team had the potential to go all the way to the championship. The season hadn't even begun, but I could tell that we were going to rock. We were destined for greatness. As the announcer called out, "The Georgia Southern Eagles!," I ran out onto the field with the rest of my team, relishing the feeling of the ever-present earth underneath me. This moment, this place, was exactly where I belonged.

The tremendous roar of the fans from the crowd was like nothing I had heard in high school. Santa Fe High had a lot of loyal supporters;

the majority of the school would show up to big games. It didn't even come close to this. Students, families, alumni, and loyal team supporters packed into the stands to see how Georgia Southern would kick off our season. The upsweep of sound was so deafening that it felt like a physical wave, capable of moving mountains.

I knew my own parents would be in the crowd somewhere, watching my first college football game. For a few futile moments, I tried to find my dad's white hat. I was no longer wearing a 9 on my jersey, but at that point it was a given that he would wear it. My eyes tried to pick out tiny details, like the bright curve of the red 9 on the front of his cap. But there were so many people in the crowd that they all seemed to mesh together into a blur. I knew in my mind that he was out there somewhere, so I settled for seeing him in my mind's eye.

The competition was a lot more intense than it had been in years past. The other team seemed far more formidable than any I had seen to date, and there were some pretty big-name guys among their ranks. For once, though, I didn't nervous. I was excited to see how well we would play together as a team, to see how well we would fare against big-name opponents. I knew that we were up for the challenge.

We took our places on the field. I looked up and furrowed my brow in concentration, staring my opponents straight in the eyes, prepared to stand my ground. I ran over the play in my head, mapping out where each footstep would fall. Then the whistle blew and the play began.

It wasn't long before I proved that I had what it takes to be an Eagle. When the ball was shoved into my hands, I took off like a shot, trying my best to get it as close to the end zone as possible. Each texturized dot of the leather ball helped me to grip it even tighter to my chest. *Keep your eyes on the end zone*, I chastised myself whenever I glanced at the chaos around me. *One step at a time, come on. Move a little faster, push harder.*

I made a beeline for the end zone, paying attention only to the thud of my feet and the pounding in my ears. My thoughts flitted to Mike and all of those long days on the playgrounds of our hometown. Before I knew it, my feet had crossed into the end zone. I stood there, numb with shock. I had scored my first collegiate TOUCHDOWN! The crowd went wild and my teammates rushed over with huge grins as I stood there, in awe of how far I had come.

We went on to finish that game, and I continued to play a major role. I scored two touchdowns that night, and I rushed a hundred and thirty yards for a spectacular finish. Not bad for a first game.

The rest of season finished remarkably well. To my surprise, I even developed following of loyal fans. Being the fullback, I received a lot of the credit for the success our team had. My coaches noticed how talented I was, and I ended up landing within the top three contestants for the Walter Payton Award during my freshman year. During my sophomore year, I was the first player of my class ranking to be honored with it. That award set me apart as the most outstanding offensive player in our division, which felt pretty darn good.

At this point, I hardly even noticed my speech impediment. I had found true friends on the team who didn't judge or complete my sentences. They wanted to hear what I had to say and always waited for it to come out. It made me think about my mom's words.

It could have always been worse.

My mom, as usual, was right. It could have been so much worse. God had his hand over my life, and I finally realized that he had heard all of my prayers, my desperate cries for help. He didn't want to take away my disability, but he wanted to put me into a place where it would no longer be as prominent. Not only that, but he was setting me up for something even greater in the future.

One Bible verse buried deep in Isaiah comes to mind: "But those who hope in the Lord will renew their strength. They will soar on wings like eagles, they will run and not grow weary, they will walk and not be faint" (Isaiah 40:3). When my dream came one step closer to being true, my strength to carry on was renewed and refreshed. As God answered my prayers, my faith in him was completely solidified and made new again. But more than that, I realized that I could run the race against my disability and still not grow weary. I was strong enough to continue fighting my disability and all of the misconceptions about me that it caused people to develop.

Perhaps even more appropriately, I realized that I was exactly where I belonged. I was a Georgia Southern Eagle, soaring past my expectations into a divine land of promise. God lifted me up on the wings of an eagle, a Georgia Southern EAGLE!

CHAPTER 9

Blessed to be a Blessing

Blessings normally come when we least expect them. When I was a scrawny seven-year-old playing football in the backyard with my brother, I hardly expected to play college football. Sure, I loved the game. I loved the way it made my heart pound, the way my feet burned with the friction of running. I even enjoyed the sweaty, sticky exhaustion certain to come after a particularly long day on the field. That moment at the end of the game when victory tastes as sweet as a cold glass of ice tea made it worthwhile. When you had to peel the clothes away from your skin at the end of the day, you knew that you had played a decent game.

I tried to give 110% to every game that came my way, but sometimes I felt like I had to give even more than usual. One day when I was coming off of a hurt ankle, my coach and teammates didn't really expect me to get into the game. "Maybe next week," the coach had said, slapping my back. Of course, I didn't listen. I sat with the physical therapist before the game, doing my stretches and trying to bear the pain and limber up. The tendons in my ankle screamed in protest as I tugged at them. It hurt, but I knew that with a proper warm-up I could still be an asset to my team that day.

I managed to run three hundred yards during that game, much to everyone's amazement. Regardless of what was going on inside of my body, I knew that my team needed to win, and I was willing to do whatever it took to show the team my dedication. From that day on,

I think the whole team took that attitude in stride. We started pushing ourselves even harder as we progressed through the season.

From the time I scored that first touchdown in my first game as an Eagle, Paulson stadium became a magical place for me. Whenever I walked in, I could hear the ringing of the metal stands as crowds stomped their feet, feel the shouts of encouragement and support. The ardor of the fans kept us on our game constantly. We didn't want to let them down.

We grew to greatness, but not without intense effort, time, and dedication. I think our secret to success had more to do with what we did off the field. For four years, I played alongside some of the guys who would later become lifelong friends. Whatever happened, we always had each other's back. When I ran down the field, I knew that someone was right behind me, trying to protect me from a tackle. We all knew what was best for each other, and we strived to work together to make it happen. And no matter how tired we were or how grueling the game had been, we always made time to grab a meal or play some games afterwards.

Even though I was the one who made most of the headlines because of my position, it was still a team game. Jealousy never threatened to tear our team apart. It was one of the most important lessons I took from my time at Georgia Southern.

As I approached senior year, I knew that I would need to face the music soon. I've always believed that there is both a starting point and an ending point to everything we do in life. When I played high school football, I didn't expect I would be able to play it forever. It was only for four years, and then I would move on to something different.

That was the moment that I began to really look into college, the starting point that brought me to where I was at that moment. It was the same thing as high school. I could play for four years, but then I had to move on to something different. It didn't matter to anyone else what I chose to do after graduation, but I couldn't stay in college for the rest of my life. It was time to graduate and begin my journey down a different avenue.

In December of my senior year, after a tremendous amount of work, I put on my rented robe and walked across the stage to receive my diploma. In my heart, I wasn't ready for it to end. I could still sit in the bleachers and feel as though the crowds were calling my name. I hadn't quite come to terms with the fact that my college days were about to fade away when something bigger began unfolding.

Four years before, I had watched as my brother was drafted into the NFL, something that only one in fifty college football players will experience. My whole family was ecstatic when the Indianapolis Colts drafted him. Imagine, the blessing of a lifetime: being drafted into the National Football League, where he could play football and get paid well to boot.

It's every kid's dream to beat the odds and play professional sports for a living. I was no exception; I badly wanted to do what I loved for a living. In the back of my mind, I was already preparing for the NFL. I was lifting weights more often, working myself harder and longer into the night to make my dream a reality. Getting into the NFL would be tough, even with my accomplishments in college football. I had won awards and broken records, but was it going to be enough to jumpstart an actual career?

After graduation I often stayed up at night, worrying and wondering about what I would do for the rest of my life. If I was meant to play in the NFL, then I knew that God would put me exactly where I needed to be. Until then, I needed to make some decisions about what I would do if I didn't get drafted that year. I had earned my degree in commercial recreation, so I tried to get things lined up. I set up interviews to work in hotels or in management. I would iron my button-down yet another time for each interview, press my dress pants until the pleat ran down the length of my leg, knot my tie over and over again until it looked perfect.

But with each smile and handshake, I knew that the corporate world wasn't really for me. I struggled to determine where I would be happy for the rest of my life if the NFL didn't work out. I would go on interviews for jobs, secretly hoping that in six months I could quit. I did end up finding a position, but it brought me no joy. I would go to work and put in my eight hours, only to rush back home to the gym to fit in a few more reps than the night before. Day by day, I could tell I was growing stronger.

When it came time for the actual draft, I drove back home so I could watch it with my parents. It was Saturday afternoon, and I found myself praying silently that my name would be called. With each new round, we got closer and closer to the edges of our seats, as if sucked forward by the gravitational pull of the television. My mom brought out plate after plate of snacks. My hands and mouth could go through the motions: pick it up, put it in my mouth, chew, swallow. But my mind was far away. We all knew that my future depended on if my name was called and by whom, but we didn't want to even think of the other option: that I would not be drafted.

Try as we might, as each team took their turn, we were all thinking it. Getting drafted into the NFL was hardly ever a sure bet. Even though I had played so well in college, it might not have been exactly what the teams were looking for this season. Maybe no one wanted a running back. Maybe no one wanted *me*.

The last round ended on Saturday and my name still hadn't been called.

We sat in silence around the television set, knowing that there were still more rounds tomorrow. It didn't necessarily mean anything that I hadn't been chosen in the first few rounds, but I didn't know if I could bear another sleepless night. My entire future depended on what would happen on that television screen in the next few days. As team owners and coaches sat around to strategize that night, would my name come up? Would anyone be thinking about whether or not they should draft Adrian Peterson?

My dad stood up and clapped me on the shoulder.

"There's tomorrow still, Adrian. They'll pick you tomorrow."

My mom agreed, musing that it seemed a bit strange that they wouldn't pick me in the first rounds but that my dad was right. There was always tomorrow.

I nodded, all silence and misery. This wasn't how I had imagined the draft going. I trudged up the stairs to my childhood room, where I had been miserable so many times before. Crawling under the covers was no longer adequate refuge, though, nor did I want it to be. I knew I had to face whatever happened, good or bad.

I tried to put things into perspective; being chosen in the first few rounds really didn't matter. I bowed my head to talk to my old friend and ask for a blessing. He was faithful, and so far he had already given me an incredible life. He would make a way for me, yet again, even if that way did not include the NFL.

"It could always be worse," I mumbled to myself as my heavy eyelids drooped and sleep threatened to pull me under.

The next morning, we gathered in the living room again. I sat uncomfortably close to the screen, so that the images warped into weird patterns in front of my strained eyes, but I didn't budge. It was as if I could force them to see me, to choose me, by sitting right in their faces. A few more rounds passed without mention of Adrian Peterson. We had already gone through five rounds when the Chicago Bears came up to have their sixth round of drafts.

The clock ticked as their time grew shorter and shorter. It seemed like a lifetime of waiting to me, even though I knew they had only taken a few short minutes. Time was running out for my name to be called, and I knew it.

"Adrian Peterson from Georgia Southern University."

As a picture of my face flashed on the screen, silence momentarily filled the room. We all sat back, stunned, that it had finally happened. All the years of work, the pressure, the games, the dedication--it had all finally paid off. We held still for a second, allowing the miracle to settle in, before giving into elation.

Our living room filled with shrieks and yells and all kinds of crazy noises. My parents' enthusiasm over having not one but two sons drafted into the NFL rang out far past our own front door, but we were in no hurry to contain ourselves.

My dream had just come true.

The NFL was a big change for me. In college, it was hard to get used to everyone being the best of the best from high school football. Now, they were the best of the best in the world. I felt intimidated at first, playing with the same people I had admired and watched on TV as a child. I was no longer playing amateur or collegiate football. I was waking up every day and going to work--which just so happened to take place on a football field.

It wasn't about how strong they were or how fast they could run. At a certain point, strength and speed plateau and then there's only so much those qualities can do for you. The NFL emphasizes detail, the tiny things that bring great plays into fruition. Skill levels were so high that they created a totally different atmosphere. My opponent might have been bigger than me or faster, but if I had better technique, I could still win. Everyone constantly tried to find creative ways to beat one other, which kept me on my game at all times.

Being drafted into the NFL was one of the greatest gifts I've ever received. I was continuously aware of how hard I had worked, and had to continue to work, to earn my place among the greatest athletes in the world. So many starry eyed kids tell their teachers they want to be professional football players when they grow up, and I had actually gone and done it! At the time, I was sure that my life was finally complete, but now I know I was missing something integral. I was missing my other half.

CHAPTER 10

My Soul Mates

While my mom tended to be a hurricane of efficiency, whirling around and never missing a beat, my dad was more like the eye of her hurricane. He was one of the strongest figures I can remember growing up. We had a fairly big family with four kids, and it tended to be a little noisy and crazy, but my dad stayed calm through every minute of the chaos. He taught us that family always came first in our household. It came before football, sleepovers, going to the movies with friends, and basketball.

From the moment I was born, my dad began teaching Mike that siblings were something to be cherished, not a nuisance. One by one, we were each taught to appreciate our siblings and our parents because family mattered most in our lives. His children meant more to him than anything in the world after his love for God and his wife.

He probably had no idea exactly what would happen to each of us as we went our separate ways. I'm sure that he never imagined that Mike and I would make it into the NFL. Parents always dream larger-than-life fantasies for their children, but watching them come true is a different story. I can still see the glittering elation in his eyes on the day that I was drafted by the Bears. His joy, and the joy of the rest of my family, made the experience so much more memorable than it already was.

My amazing, tight-knit experience growing up made me badly want to have my own kids. I had been raised with so much life and vibrancy that my lonely apartment seemed sad in comparison. I pictured going to my own children's football games and basketball games, teaching them to read, watching them walk across the stage at their high school graduation. It seemed to be the one thing that I didn't have. I wanted children so that I could give them the same opportunities that I had received, so I could raise them the same way that my father had raised me.

Throughout college, that dream seemed distant. Once in a while my mind would flip back to that fantasy and I would imagine falling asleep next to my wife or waking up to my child tugging my arm. I dated a few girls here and there, but none of them held my attraction or my interest enough for me to consider something serious. Until Angela came along.

It was the spring of my junior year, and it seemed like the perfect time for love. Whenever the flowers bloom and blazing heat finally emerges from a tepid winter, new relationships seem to grow. All over the Georgia Southern campus, new couples walked around with their fingers interlaced. It seemed like a scene out of a movie, one that I didn't belong in just yet.

I had met Angela a few times through friends. She was a student at Georgia Southern too, a freshmen. She was beautiful and funny, and I decided to take a chance and ask her out on a date. Much to my surprise, she said yes. We set a date and time and I walked away bewildered. I worried a little bit about stumbling over my words, but more than anything else, I hoped she would try to see past my disability and give me a chance to finish my sentences.

The night of our date came, and I had to admit that for the first time in a while I was nervous. I had painstakingly selected my outfit, all the while surprised at the things I found myself doing to impress her. The minute I picked her up, though, I realized that it was worth the trouble. She looked incredible and I could hardly take my eyes off of her the entire night.

I didn't realize it then, but Angela had captured my heart.

We continued to see each other over the next six months or so because I could never get enough of her. I wanted her by my side all the time. She was fun to be around, and when I was with her, the pressures of college seemed to float away.

But I knew that I would graduate in just a few months, and that the next semester I would be gone, training for the NFL draft. Angela would still attend Georgia Southern. If we wanted to continue seeing each other, we would have to establish a long-distance relationship. I was not enthusiastic about the prospect. It would be hard not to have her by my side all the time, available to go on a date with me every Friday night. She wouldn't be able to come to my football games in the fall, and it might be hard just to schedule a phone call with her. Plus, we knew that those kinds of relationships had a low success rate. Despite the difficulties, we both decided that it would be best for us if we at least attempted a long-distance relationship. We had only been together for six months, but we were fairly serious about each other and we wanted to be able to say that we had tried.

We did try, and it worked. We talked regularly, Angela always the same fun girl that I remembered from our first date. For six years, we continued to keep our relationship going. We even managed to fall in love. It was so much more than we had imagined it could be.

It took a lot of growing up on my part to finally step up and ask her to marry me. It wasn't some momentous decision. Our love had come along gradually, creeping into our lives one laugh at a time, and I had to wait for the perfect moment. I didn't want to rush the decision because I knew that marriage was a lifelong commitment. It felt that one quick move could shatter all of the years of hard work we put into coming this far, so I waited. Even after we had dated for several years, Angela was just graduating college and getting her life together. I had moved to Chicago a few years earlier, and she was moving back home to be near her family.

So a few more years passed, we grew up a lot, and eventually the timing was just right.

As I got ready to propose, I thought about the path that had led me to Angela. I had always mysteriously been better at talking to girls than boys, and on top of that I had been blessed with a woman who saw past my disability into my soul. I realized it was because God had always wanted me to create a family of my own. It felt as though Angela had been made specifically for me.

I still remember the day Angela told me we were going to be parents. It was mid-season and I was coming and going from home between games and trips. Angela couldn't even wait until I got home to share the news with me. I was in my hotel room one night, just about to call her, when I noticed that she was one step ahead of me. I leisurely listened to the jingle of my ringtone as I pulled the phone out and answered.

"Hey," I said, happy just to hear her voice. We tried to talk for at least a few minutes each night when I was on the road like this. It hurt so much to be apart, but we both knew it would happen. The separation was really nothing new for us after six years in a long-distance relationship, but that factor didn't alleviate the loneliness.

"I have something to tell you. I was going to wait until you came home, but I really just can't do that," she rambled. At first I feared that maybe something was wrong, but then I heard the smile in her voice.

"What is it, baby?" I asked.

"We're having a baby!" she yelled.

We were having a baby? At first, it was hard for me to even wrap my head around being a father. It was something I had always wanted, but I didn't know what would happen now. I was always on the road, and I would hardly be there to help Angela and take part in my kid's life. I wanted so badly to live up to the example that my own father had set for me. I was over the moon with happiness, but inside I felt a tight ball of nerves start to form like a pearl inside an oyster.

Angela and I celebrated over the phone, making plans and talking about what life might be like once our child was born. Eventually the night grew darker and we had to say goodbye, but we knew that our reunion would be incredible.

I'm going to be a dad, I thought as I lay under the rough sheets of my hotel bed. There was so much responsibility that came with being a father, and I wasn't sure that I was really ready for all that was going to come after. I knew that my dad had been an incredible role model. I should have had no fears at all; all I had to do was follow the example he had shown me time and time again. But soon a small life would depend on me to protect it, to provide for it, to care for it and love it. Was I really ready for that kind of responsibility, no matter how badly I might have wanted it? Eventually, I settled in under stiff blankets, breathing in the smell of industrial-strength bleach that permeated from them. Certainly everyone had those same fears and worries, but I knew it would work out. I closed my eyes and fell asleep with a smile on my face. My final dream was coming true.

Months later, I was home, and Angela and I had just gotten back from yet another prenatal appointment. Nearing the end of her pregnancy, we both felt ready for our son to arrive. I was sitting on the couch, trying to quell my fears about being a father. I could handle having huge football players chasing after me on the field, but could I handle caring for a child?

I didn't have much time to think about it because just then, Angela announced that her water had broken.

My heart started to pound unnaturally fast. There wasn't much time. I needed to get her to the hospital, I needed to get her bag, I needed to find the car keys. I hated seeing Angela in pain, and in the frenzy of trying to get everything together, I was clumsier than usual. Angela tried her best to be patient with me, but each contraction that tore through her body made things harder. I remember finally speeding away from the house, my hands gripping the steering wheel so tightly I thought it might snap in two.

As we pulled up to the hospital, I let her out at the emergency room doors, parked the car, and sprinted back as fast as my football training would allow. I grabbed hold of Angela's arm and helped her inside, where we were greeted by a nurse with a wheelchair. A wave of relief swept over me: we had made it to the hospital. I knew that she was now in good hands.

The nurse pushed her back into the maternity ward while another woman handed me a stack of paperwork to fill out. I dutifully scribbled answer after answer, digging around in my wallet for insurance cards and jotting down numbers and policies. In a way I was grateful to have something calming and mind-numbing to do, since it kept me from thinking about what was happening back in the maternity ward.

"A doctor will call you back in a little bit, sir," the receptionist told me when I handed her the completed pile.

In a little bit? What was I going to do until then? I sat back down in the chair, but I couldn't manage to sit still. I kept tapping my hands on my knees and shaking my legs around until other patrons started giving me funny looks. I didn't care who stared at me, though. All I wanted was to be with my wife. Frustrated and fidgety, I got up and stalked around the waiting area until I found a vending machine. I sank my hands deep into my pockets, searching for the spare change to buy another distraction. Each coin made a nasty *clunk* as it entered the machine, but the sound did not drown out my thoughts. I surveyed the snack options as if I was making an important life decision, weighing the difference between peanut butter crackers and cheese crackers.

I wonder if Angela is okay... if our baby is okay...

I sat down in the quiet waiting room to eat, feeling horribly out of place. The crinkle of the wrapper and the pop of the top on my can of soda made everyone look condescendingly in my direction. I tried to keep quiet, but each crunch brought more stares of disapproval. With a sigh, I tossed the crackers into the trash can. I wasn't hungry anyway.

I held my soda in one hand and flipped absentmindedly through a gossip magazine. I soon realized that I did not care what it said. I felt like I was going crazy, so I stepped to a quieter part of the waiting room to call my dad.

"Hey, son. How's it going?" he asked as he picked up the phone.

"It's good. Listen, I'm in the hospital right now. Angela's having the baby," I said as quietly as I could. I could still hear the desperation in my voice though.

"Are you nervous?" he asked knowingly. I nodded and he seemed to get the message, even though he couldn't see me.

"It's all right. Everyone's nervous when they have their first kid, Adrian. You'll be fine. You'll see."

I sure hoped so. I thanked him and let him go, then tried to resume waiting in silence. I sat back in my seat and closed my eyes, trying not to imagine all of the things that could go wrong. It felt like hours had passed when I finally heard someone call my name.

"Adrian, would you like to come on back now? Your wife's ready to see you."

I jumped out of my chair so fast that it nearly fell over. It was time for me to see my wife, and soon it would be time for me to meet my son. I followed the nurse back, silently willing him to walk just a little bit faster. He seemed to stroll along as slowly as possible, and it was driving me insane. Even at that snail's pace, though, we made it to the room. I rushed in to see Angela without a second thought.

As soon as I saw her face, I knew that I had no reason to fear anything. Despite her pain, she had a certain glow about her that comforted me. One look at her and I knew everything was going to be all right, even in all of the uncertainty.

Hours passed and her contractions came closer and closer together. I no longer had the panicked feeling that had overcome me in the waiting room. I just wanted to be there for Angela. She gripped my hand tightly as each contraction came, making me think that my fingers would snap like twigs. I knew, though, that the pain in my hand was absolutely nothing compared to what she felt.

"It's time!" the doctor announced, a huge smile on her face. "Let's get you to push, Angela. Are you ready?"

It felt like an eternity that she was screaming beside me, panting hard to try to catch her breath in the midst of the effort and pain. I felt helpless in the face of her pain, but I knew all I could do was hold her hand and pray to God that everything turned out fine. Finally, I heard an unfamiliar cry, and my heart leapt. I tried not to look toward the blood- and fluid-soaked end of the bed, but I couldn't help it. I wanted to see my son.

My eyes went directly to him. His tiny little body was huddled up on the scale as the doctor inspected him. The nurse gently picked him up and smiled as she carried him over to Angela to hold for the first time. Nothing could beat that image in my mind. My wife holding our firstborn--something we had waited for so long. It was a lifelong dream come to fruition.

When they handed him to me, I could feel this tiny life settling into my arms. I was scared I would drop him, break his fragile body, but everyone assured me that it would be fine. Here was my first child. I had helped to create him, and he was going to count on me for the next twenty years or so. Even now, when I was well beyond the age when my dad was obligated to take care of me, I had still called him from the waiting room when I was freaking out. He was my rock, and I knew that would change. Now it was my turn to be someone's rock.

I had become a father myself.

I felt a tear roll down my cheek, and I let it stay there. No one said anything about it. The medical staff soon took our boy for cleaning and shots, and I waited beside Angela's bed, her fingers laced with mine. As I brushed a tendril of sweaty hair from one of her eyes, she smiled at me.

"We did it," she said. "We finally have a family."

We took Adrian home only a few days later. We learned things the hard way, just like every new parent does. We didn't have nannies and babysitters to help us, and most of our family members lived too far away to come over daily to help us get things set up and organized. The hard work, though, was well worth it. We were sleep-deprived and deliriously happy, and it was amazing to watch Adrian progress through every little milestone and giggle and drool his way through the first part of his life.

It seemed that no time at all had passed before I was explaining to Adrian how to be a big brother. I tried to teach him the same things that my parents had taught me about loving younger siblings, helping them, and playing with them. I wanted him to cherish his family and have the same bond that I had with my brothers and sister. When Aaden finally arrived, we worried about how Adrian would react to having another little boy in the house. Our fears turned out to be unfounded. He took to him immediately, asking to hold him and carry him around. He would ask if he could hold the bottle while Aaden drank and would spend countless hours sitting on the floor playing with Aaden until he learned to walk. The fondness was mutual: Aaden cried with his brother wasn't in the room with him.

One day, as we watched the kids tussle on the floor, Angela and I sat on the couch and smiled at each other. I put my arm around her shoulders and knew that we had made the right decision in having another child. The two of them were already building a bond that would last forever. I suddenly realized that this must have been how my dad felt watching Mike and me grow up. We remain close even now, talking regularly and reminiscing about our younger days. I was seeing that kind of friendship come to life in a whole new generation. My life felt full--full of joy, full of contentment, and full of blessings. But I still had one more blessing to come.

"Are you sure, Angela?" I asked, hardly wanting to believe that it was true.

"I'm positive," she told me. Sure enough, she was right. We were pregnant for a third time. As before, we made all of the doctor appointments and she took her prenatal vitamins. Once again, we talked to the boys about what it meant to be older siblings, how to take care of a baby, and what the new addition would mean for our family. We had no idea at the time that this pregnancy would be different.

At sixteen weeks, we went in for our ultrasound.

"Are you ready to know what the sex of your baby is?" the doctor asked, smiling.

I grabbed Angela's hand and we nodded.

"It looks like you guys are having a girl! Congratulations!"

Our first baby girl. I could already imagine that she would be just like her mother. Our family would be complete with two boys and a girl. I could take the boys to football practices and practice with them on the weekends, and I would also have a little girl to spoil shamelessly. We felt as though we were walking on clouds as we baby-proofed the house in preparation for our upcoming arrival.

As the days and months wore on, I could see Angela's stomach growing larger. She had to switch back to maternity clothes and big t-shirts in order to accommodate our baby. She was beautiful during this pregnancy, just as she had been during previous ones. Everything seemed to be perfect until we hit the six-month mark and went in for another ultrasound.

"I think there's something wrong with the baby," the doctor confessed, her voice low and sad.

Angela and I sat in silence, not wanting to believe that it could be true. How could it be? Everything was going so well, and we were about to have our little girl. She had to be healthy, she just had to be.

Slowly, the doctor drew pictures of our child's kidneys up on the screen, pointing to bits of white that the untrained eye wouldn't even notice.

"Do you see these here? These are cysts on her left kidney, several of them. Without a properly functioning kidney, she might never be able to enjoy life the way a normal child would. But that's not the biggest problem that I see here," she warned.

I could hardly take in any more information. My eyes were watering, and Angela was already crying as silently as possible. *Not the brain*, I thought as the doctor began to move towards the top of the ultrasound. *I'd rather her just have a deformity than have something wrong with her brain.*

The doctor solemnly stood up to point out something on the screen. As her finger gravitated toward the baby's head, my stomach dropped. If I had been standing, I'm sure that my knees would have given out because in that moment, the only thing I wanted to do was to cry out.

"These here are calcium stems on her brain."

She continued to explain what that meant for the baby, but it didn't register with me. I was still having a difficult time processing what it would mean for her to have a brain problem. Would she be able to walk and talk like other children? I felt a lump as big as an egg form in my throat, and tears began to run unchecked down my face.

"Your best option may be to abort the pregnancy."

I looked at Angela, who had completely lost all control of her emotions. I felt powerless to help her as we sat there and cried together, mourning the loss of something that had yet to come. I'm not sure how long we sat like that, but eventually we knew that we had to leave the office. We wanted time to sort through our emotions and our options in the privacy of our own home.

On the car ride home, I feared that I would get into a crash because of my blurred vision. I couldn't keep the tears away long enough to focus on my surroundings. Angela sat beside me, still sobbing. Somehow we made it back to the house and into our room, where we collapsed on the bed. We were so far into the pregnancy and we had made so many plans for what would happen when this baby was born. We had even picked out a name: Amelia. And the doctor was telling us that it would be best to forget all of those plans, to forget about Amelia, and to abort her.

"We can't abort her, Adrian," Angela sobbed. "She's a living human being."

She was right. We had always placed our faith in God to protect us, to take care of us. In our eyes, aborting this pregnancy would be killing our little girl.

"But what about what the doctor said? She might never have a real life. She could just easily die right after she's born," I argued. I didn't want to give up on my dream of having a little girl, but I wanted to take what the doctors thought into consideration too. Would it be best to abort her? Would carrying Amelia to term leave Angela's life in danger?

Angela just shook her head, tears streaming down her face. I had never seen her this upset, this devastated before. She grabbed for my hands and bowed her head, and I knew exactly what she was asking me to do. I closed my eyes and took a deep breath to lift up a prayer. My heart was breaking as I laid our situation before God and asked for his mercy and his grace. I begged for the wisdom to make the right decision and pleaded for him to bless us for being faithful to him. I asked that he would take this cup of suffering from us, that we would go back for another ultrasound in two weeks and those ailments would be gone. We were asking for a miraculous healing.

Two weeks passed by slowly, as if we were just inching along. We still had two boys to take care of, and we didn't want them to know exactly what was going on. I could hardly sleep. I would wake up in the middle of the night just to watch Angela breathing. In a way I felt like her guardian, as if by staring at her for long enough I could fix what was wrong with our infant. My eyelids would tug, fighting for release, but in my grief I maintained my vigil. I felt completely powerless over the entire situation. God was directing this show, and I was merely a spectator, praying for the ending to be a happy one.

We continued to pray that same prayer each night. It became clear to us after a time that God was saying we should carry her to full term. We were not to abort this baby. It wasn't our right to decide whether or not she should live or die. If she didn't survive past birth, it was God's job to call her home, not ours.

The next appointment came, and we sat in the chair, still silently praying that God had performed a miracle. When the pictures came up on the screen again, I felt as though we had been betrayed. God wasn't listening. He didn't heal our baby girl.

"Have you made a decision about what to do yet?" the doctor asked, trying to be gentle about the situation.

"We're going to carry her to full term," Angela said. In that moment, we both felt an incredible peace wash over us. We had made the right decision.

We came home that day, certain that everything was going to take care of itself, but we still worried, and waited. Three months was a long time to be in limbo, unsure of exactly where things were going and what we would be able to do. My worry grew right along with Angela's stomach as the months passed. It was unlike anything that I had ever had to deal with before. I couldn't go to the weight room and work harder to heal Amelia. It wasn't something that I could lift and train for. I constantly felt I wasn't big enough for the problems that had been thrown our way.

In many ways, I related to Peter on the day that he walked on the water to Christ. There had been a large storm, and the disciples were gathered on the boat waiting on Jesus to return. They couldn't go any further ahead because the waves continually pressed them back, but they couldn't return to the shore because the sea was too choppy behind them. They panicked, unsure of what to do with their lives on the line. Then they looked out over the water and noticed someone walking towards them.

Peter called out, asking Jesus if he could come walk on the water with him.

"Come to me," Jesus answered, and Peter took that first hesitant step onto the water. Much to his surprise, it supported his weight. However, with the second step, he began to sink and called out to Jesus to save him.

"Why did you doubt?" came Jesus's answer.

I felt a lot like Peter. God had placed Angela and me in the midst of this incredible storm. We were broken and tired, uncertain of what we should do next. But God was coming and we begged him to let us come to him. He told us to save Amelia, but we still felt as though we were drowning. I could feel God asking us why we doubted his plan.

We decided that we would rather take chances with God on our side. We were going to finish this pregnancy and take care of our baby, no matter what happened. We would stick by our faith. There was no rehearsal, no practice session. This was just life, coming at us, and we had to make the best of it.

On the day Angela's water broke, we went through the motions of getting her to the hospital again. I felt nervous this time, but not nearly in the same way I had been for Adrian's birth.

Would my little girl live?

Three months of impatience, of wondering and not knowing what would happen were finally coming to an end. I sat with Angela as she held my hand in silence. We were a team. No matter what happened that day, nothing could change that.

The minute Amelia came into the world, screaming, I knew that everything was as it should be. The nurses handed her to us, and we just wanted to hold her for hours, admiring her precious face, her tiny hands, and her beautiful eyes.

We had almost given up on her, and yet here she was in my arms. She was alive, and everything was going to be fine. In the end, she only needed to stay in the hospital for an extra ten days before we could finally bring her home. God had been on our side, fighting for us. Why had we ever doubted that things would work out?

After all, we had seen plenty of blessings from him. Why would our little girl be any different?

CHAPTER 11

The Run of My Life

As I sit here in the ever-approaching twilight of my football career, I can't help but think back to that day, the day of the national championship game in Chattanooga, Tennessee, against Youngstown State University. The screams of thousands of fans echoed through the air, cheering me and the rest of the Eagles on so we could take home yet another championship trophy. I didn't know if I would be ready for the game after coming off my injury, but as it turned out, I made one of the biggest plays of my entire career that day.

That play was titled simply "the run" by analysts after watching the video over and over again, but I remember it much differently. I remember the ball vibrating in my hands as the quarterback turned around and handed it to me. I remember catching just a glimpse of where I needed to go before obstacle after obstacle blocked my view. I promised myself that I would run through them, one by one, until I reached that finish line.

When the first Youngstown player tried to take me down, adrenaline began pumping through my veins. I couldn't and wouldn't give in. I pushed him out of the way as another player latched onto my back. Spinning around, I continued to run, energy surging through me. I caught the flash of a red jersey in my peripheral vision, and I reached out to grab hold of it and threw the player down, past the sidelines, as if to tell him that he would not stop me. I pushed the next opponent to the ground as well and kept running until the final Youngstown player barreled toward me. The full weight of his body made me turn and stumble as I slammed into the ground, my precious cargo clutched tightly to my chest.

The referee threw down his yellow flag and my run officially ended, just one yard short of a touchdown.

As I sit here and watch this tape again with my beautiful wife by side and three amazing children running around the house, I'm amazed by how far I've come over the years. The ability to run like that didn't come because I wanted it to. It came because, days upon days and years upon years, I had prepared for that moment. I prepared to run through obstacles and past objections that my disability brought on. When the crowd cheered on that day, I cheered along with them. I knew I had finally conquered my own self-doubt and fear of failure. I hoped that somewhere in that screaming crowd, someone with the same shortcomings that I had felt liberated.

As a child, I thought that I would never be able to move past my stutter. For years it formed the core of who I was because I allowed it to define what I would and would not be able to accomplish. I gave in to the myth that rising above a disability is impossible. While it was true that I couldn't control my stutter, I didn't have to let it limit my options and my life. Even now, I'm reaping the rewards of not letting it get in my way.

I had run past the Youngstown State players, never letting them pin me to the ground. I ran right past them without a second thought. In the interviews before the game, one of the Youngstown players had given plenty of quotes about his determination to take me down during the game. In the end, when he came close to me, I was able to grab him by his jersey and toss him aside. Nothing could stop me from doing what I wanted to do.

After everything I had been through, those obstacles, those players I had to get through were absolutely *nothing*. The minute I stood up on the field again, it was so rewarding to see the things I had worked for my entire life become a reality. I had the greatest run of my entire career, but perhaps my most important run was the one against myself.

I had run past Doubt, directly through the war my disability had waged on my spirit. It threatened to take me down and hold me there, but I couldn't let it. It wanted to pin me to the ground until it crushed me into a heap of dying ember, certain to never flame again.

But I didn't let it.

What my mom told me that night I sat sniffling on the edge of the bathtub was right. It could have always been worse. There was no sense in sitting around feeling sorry for myself, because I had been blessed with incredible talent and possibility. I could choose to let my stutter hold me back from doing the things that I dreamed of, or I could choose to fight against it. That night, I made the decision to fight.

Over the years, I continued to battle myself. After all, Doubt doesn't stay down for long: you have to constantly fight against it. I cringed as kids teased me in school, I watched as my brother cast a shadow that seemed impossibly long, I sweated and panicked through standardized tests. But I never backed down, and I was able to run directly past my disability and into the sweetest place in the world, one filled with promise and possibilities.

Speaking will never be my strongest attribute. I was told that I would never be able to speak like normal kids at a very young age. But then I learned that greatness isn't found in words, but in deeds. The minute that I stopped looking only at the things I was struggling with, I began to see the activities at which I really excelled.

Before the world can stop focusing on your shortcomings, you have to set an example. A disability is a part of you, but it does not have to define who you are or who you will be. I'm convinced that nobody's disabilities should hold them back from experiencing their dreams.

There is *always* a way to get around your opponent. Most often, the disability isn't even our biggest threat. Our biggest threat is our fear of being ourselves. We spend so much time focusing on our weaknesses that we never give ourselves a chance to see our strengths. Self-doubt is a disability on its own, but one we can rise above.

All of us have our demons. Yours may be an actual disability or an insecurity, but no matter what form it takes, it doesn't have to limit you. You're only limited when you refuse to use your imagination to see a way around it. It might mean that you have to work a little harder or do things differently than you had planned. But wouldn't it be worth it if you could one day say that you had beaten the odds?

Stop defining yourself by your disability. Instead, remind yourself that you should never dis your abilities. Look at what you're good at. See what you could be great at. Search inside yourself and figure out what you want to do with your life, then get out there and find a way. Start looking at the positive things and give yourself permission to do the impossible. Give yourself permission to be great.

That run against Youngstown may have been the best day of my career, but it was also the ultimate symbol of my determination to succeed. When I rose up from the grass at the end of my run and looked around, I realized the truth. I finally said to myself and to everyone around me that they would *never* be able to dis my abilities again.